# the Techniques Series:
# Rhythm & Percussion

## Rhythm & Percussion

**Photographs by:** James Cumptsy, Music Maker Publications plc
**Printed by:** Staples of Rochester, Kent.
**Copyright:** Music Maker Publications plc.
**Designed by:** David Houghton
**Published by:** Castle Communications plc, A29 Barwell Business Park,
Leatherhead Road, Chessington, Surrey KT9 2NY.

While the publishers have made every reasonable effort to trace the copyright
owners for any or all photographs in this book, there may be some omissions of
credits for which we apologise.

**ISBN:** 1-86074-146-0

# the Techniques Series:
# Rhythm & Percussion

compiled & edited by
**Ronan Macdonald**

# contents

# foreword

There's no denying the calibre of artists who have graced the pages of *Rhythm* magazine. Everyone who is anyone has shared their ideas, knowledge and views with us in the ten years plus that *Rhythm* has been around. However, a lot of credit for the success and character of the magazine is due to the many and varied subjects covered alongside our favourite drummers and percussionists. From dhol drumming to pub drumming, practice, studio or conga techniques... If it's a Ludwig Vistalite you're interested in, somewhere down the line it's been covered. I've always been a sucker for anything vintage, so Bob Henrit's lovingly compiled reports on the current market value of a Rogers Dynasonic or Trixon teardrop bass drum have always been a favourite of mine.

*Rhythm* has consistently covered, for want of a better word, ethnic drumming with insight, hopefully reminding you and me that the language of drumming is relative and relevant to anybody who aspires to play as well as he or she possibly can. And recently, the addition of the *Beats Working* supplement has seen *Rhythm's* educational content go from strength to strength.

As a contributor myself, with, amongst other things, the report on the *Help* album of 1995, I have always found *Rhythm* eager to broaden the outlook of all its readers. Here in this book are some of the best of those features, gleaned and compiled by Ronan Macdonald. Put down your sticks for half an hour and enjoy...

**Steve White**

# introduction

## So You Want To Play Drums?

What's so great about drums then? And why should anyone want to start playing them? Well, put it this way: Ringo Starr. Once just the prominently proboscised sticksman in Rory Storm And The Hurricanes with no more lofty ambition than to open a hairdressing salon, Mr. Grumpy went on to enjoy considerable success with a band called The Beatles, ended up a very rich man indeed, and married ex-Bond girl Babara Bach. Way to go, big nose! Or take Tico Torres — who you may or may not know as Bon Jovi's un-oil painting-like beatmonger. He left his not exactly soaring career as a roofer in New Jersey to find fame and fortune in the wacky world of rock 'n' roll. Several squillion albums and a few world tours later, he's divorced from Brooke Shields, engaged to supermodel Eva Herzigova, and, again, not exactly strapped for cash. And then there's Phil Collins: one-time knitwear catalogue model, young Phil hit the big time as the only member of Genesis who didn't go to public school, and ended up richer than all of them put together. Probably. He's now Britain's highest paid company chairman or something and — oh yes — he plays the drums.

Quite apart from all that, you've seen *Top Of The Pops* — who looks like they're having the best time? Who's the one at the back giving it loads and looking totally cool doing it? Who's the one responsible for the beat that everyone's dancing to? Who's the one the girls/boys all fancy? It is — you guessed it — the drummer. (Unless it's a drum machine of course, but that's another story.)

Of all the families of musical instruments, percussion is the most immediately satisfying. You may have sat behind a drum kit before, in which case you don't need me to tell you how much fun it is just flailing about mindlessly and making a big racket. But would you be surprised to learn that any half decent teacher could teach you how to play a basic rock pattern, perfectly usable with a band, in about fifteen minutes tops? And you can take drumming to any level you want: you don't have to be able to read music or know the first thing about music theory. Hell, if you just want to be in a band you can teach yourself — simply put on a record featuring a piece of (simple) drumming you like and try to copy it. But, if you're prepared to put the hours in, the drums can be one of the most technically

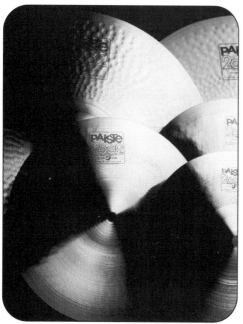

✪ Drums, Cymbals and sticks: your first step towards becoming monstrously cool.

demanding and rewarding of instruments to learn, with its own equivalent of scales and arpeggios in the form of rudiments, which is the next of many levels.

So whaddya reckon? Fancy giving it a go? Well, I haven't been totally honest with you — you do need certain qualifications to play the drums. Sorry.

First of all, you need limbs. You don't even need all four, as long as you've got most of them you'll be okay. You also need to be able to move each one independently of the others, which sounds impossibly difficult but actually isn't. Honest.

Secondly, you need to be able to count. To four. Sometimes you'll need to be able to wrestle with really big numbers like seven. Or even twelve!

Thirdly: a sense of rhythm. This is the one most people worry about, but if you have a heartbeat then you have a sense of rhythm. You do have a heartbeat, don't you?

Fourthly: a brain. As with most things in life, this is a prerequisite for success. If you have no brain then try playing bass or something. (This is a 'musician's joke'; a whole new vista of rib-shattering 'comedy' that will become open to you as soon as you buy your first kit. Great, eh?)

Finally: suitable clothing. You must, repeat must own a muscle vest. You must never, repeat never wear it. Every drummer, I'm afraid to say, owns at least one muscle vest (preferably with a rising sun design on it), but only the saddest of the sad will ever actually wear it.

And that really is all you need to pick up a pair of sticks and start playing the drums. Obviously what I'm trying to tell you is that anyone can do this, there's no such thing as an unnatural drummer. Ringo is frequently cited as technically one of the worst drummers of all time, but he hasn't exactly done badly for himself, has he? American drummers in particular burst

many blood vessels in their attempts to pay homage to the loveable mop-top (with the very large nose). Also, it must be said, half the drumming you hear on the radio nowadays is at least indirectly influenced by his groundbreaking style.

Okay, so you've decided to give it a go, this drumming lark, and you need to know what to do about equipment. Well, there are three options available to you: buy a new drum kit, buy a second hand drum kit off a member of the public, or buy a second hand drum kit from a shop.

Let's take the last option first, since it's by far the least complicated. Work out exactly how much you've got to spend and find a shop that deals in second hand drums. This way you get professional advice on what your best buy is, as well as someone to go back and complain to should anything go wrong. If it's your first kit though (which if you're reading this and taking any of it in, it presumably is), it's a good idea to take someone with you who knows about drums so you don't end up buying a turkey.

The other way, which is generally cheaper, is to look through the small ads in your local paper, or a drum magazine such as *Rhythm*. However, while this allows for a certain amount of haggling and some very good bargains, you don't have the security of being able to do anything about it if you discover a crack in a shell or whatever.

Generally though, with the right advice, taking the second hand option can result in the ownership of a high quality setup for the same price as a kit of lower quality.

But what if you're into buying things new? If you wouldn't be seen dead playing anything that had been touched before by mortal hand (and, indeed, foot) then you have a huge choice of kits before you. The true starter kit should weigh in at between £250 and £300. However, if you're really serious about things and can afford it, the next level (between £450 and £600) is represented by kits such as the Pearl Export and Premier APK, both of which are best-sellers. Whichever option you go for, one thing cannot be avoided, and that is the need for decent heads (that's 'skins' in layman's terms) on one's kit. This takes some experimentation since there are now quite a few different makes and models on the market, and you need to find the ones that are right for you. Second hand won't really do here I'm afraid — heads definitely need to be in at least very good condition. Oh, and you never get a stool included with any new kit, so shop around. Most drum manufacturers sell cheap stools as well as the more expensive models. Don't feel you need to spend a fortune on seating at this stage, take whatever's most comfortable within your budget. Phil Collins still uses a bottom of the range Premier stool that must be pushing twenty years old.

And it doesn't end there — you need cymbals. Again, going for second hand stuff here can be a good money-saving idea, but with cymbals even more than drums you do need to check that what you're shelling out for is in good working order. The slightest crack or warp should be enough to dissuade you from buying unless the price is extremely low — even then, you should never touch a cracked cymbal with a barge pole. As far as new cymbals go, the biggies such as Zildjian, Sabian and Paiste all have starter packs which usually comprise a crash, a ride and a pair of hi-hats retailing at somewhere between £100 and £150. However, less well known companies like Meinl and Camber actually specialise in economical cymbals and are most definitely worth checking out.

Your final expense will be sticks. As with heads, you need to make the right choice for you. There are endless different sizes, lengths and weights of stick, so try them out until you find a model you're totally comfortable with. And don't be fooled into

thinking that the drumstick bargain bin in your local music shop means you'll never have to spend more than three quid on a pair of sticks — it won't take you long to realise that sticks really do need to be perfectly straight and evenly weighted.

That's basically it as far as equipment goes. Apart from the fact that you probably can't play the drums yet, you are a drummer. But a drummer is nothing without a band...

It's all very well sitting in your bedroom all day setting musical fire to your drum kit, but unless you're in a band, what's the point? Remember, you're playing the drums to be the coolest person on earth, and how can you possibly do that unless you're playing in front of other people?

The question you need to ask yourself is: what sort of music do I want to play? This is an easy one — simply look through your record collection and work it out.

Next, find a band. Unless you have a burning desire to play avant garde free jazz, there's probably a band already out there looking for you. Keep an eye on the 'Musicians Wanted' sections in publications such as *Melody Maker*, *NME*, *Rhythm*, *Guitarist* etc. and you're certain to eventually find a band looking for a drummer, hopefully in your area. It's even worth trying your local newspaper.

Bear in mind that at this stage you don't want to get involved in anything too advanced. If you've literally just started playing then ignore anything that includes the words 'gigs waiting', 'very experienced' or 'professional'. I'm sure you get the idea. Established bands know what they're looking for, they hold auditions, and if you've only been playing for weeks it's going to be a waste of your time and theirs, not to mention potentially humiliating. So look for a band that's just starting out, or something where technical ability is unimportant.

Probably the best way for the novice

✪ **Phil Collins**

musician to join a band, however, is to get some mates together and start one him or herself. The advantages are obvious: you're working with people you already know, everyone's going to be straight with each other right from the start, and there's (hopefully) less chance for musical differences to rear their ugly heads.

The majority of drummers are perfectly happy playing in a band and progressing technically on their own, perhaps using books, videos, or other learning aids. Others take things more seriously, perhaps setting their sights on drumming as a career, or simply wanting to be the best they can be. These people are going to need tuition, which, unsurprisingly, can be arrived at by one of two paths. Private teachers generally put their own ads up in

music shops (many shops actually have their own on-site teaching studios), schools and so on. Premier Percussion also run a database containing hundreds of drum and percussion teachers in the UK, which is well worth getting hold of. The other path leads back to school. Although this may surprise you, there are two major drum schools in London: Drumtech and the Percussion Institute of Technology. Both places offer year-long full-time courses as well as part-time ones and single lessons. Obviously places are limited and auditions necessary, but it does lead to a real qualification in drumming.

Well, that's all you really need to know to get started. Remember, you can take your drumming to any level you want — that's the whole point. It can be as simple or advanced as you choose to make it, and either way, you can still have a practical place in the mystical, magical, marvellous world of music. And that, as you'll soon discover, is one of the many reasons why drumming is great.

# chapter 1
# Dazed And Confused

Drumming is a pretty straightforward business, isn't it? Set up the stuff and off you go. But the drummer is beset by a wealth of options for just what 'stuff' he sets up, almost an embarrassment of choices. There are dark cymbals. Heavy cymbals ("We sell a lot of them 'cos they say heavy on them," says the helpful assistant). Medium cymbals. Bright heads. Dull heads. Piccolo snares. Steel or brass, sir? Just imagine cymbals 30 years ago: a big one, a small one and the hi-hats. Progress is fantastic. We're spoilt for choice. And then once we've made all our lovely choices, we get the gear home/on stage/to the arena/into the studio and it sounds nothing like you imagined it. You hear it through the monitor or on the tape, and you think, "That doesn't sound like me, surely? What's going on? That cymbal's meant to be dark... Didn't I tune those toms higher than that? What the hell is going on?" Or as drumming legend Uncle Peter would say, "Where am I? Donkey!"

You see, I'm confused. In the last three years I've had as many ride cymbals. My problem is that, finally able to afford the top of the range and spending ages in the shop playing so many wonderful hand-hammered, computer-contoured, smoke-cured cymbals, none of which I could fault, I found myself lost. I've only ever played cheap cymbals before. Trying to sound knowledgeable, I mutter something about a dark cymbal, am directed to a 'dark' cymbal, and find out what they mean by 'dark'. The vocabulary and my ears are starting to fail me. They all sound great, they all sound crap. I don't know what they sound like any more. Now, what you're supposed to do is bring in your other 'metals' and compare and contrast. You might even bring in your drums to aid you in choosing the tastiest cymbal for the job. Better still, get the band in and have them play so you can find out which lucky saucepan lid gets the vote. But I play in four bands. Does that mean I need four cymbals? Whoa there! This is all getting out of hand, so to help make up my mind, I look to see who uses what, and the endorsement comes to the rescue. I like this guy's playing, he always sounds great; I trust his judgement and plump for the star model. After all, they're all so certain about 'their sound', aren't they? So no reason it won't work for me. Then I get home and in my bedroom with my drums...

The root of the problem goes back to the whole PA/recording thing. When the endorsee plays his cymbal in the studio, it may not be the same model as the one in

○ A cymbal assortment

the advert. A simple case of mistaken identity. Harder to compensate for is the fact that what you hear on your walkman or stereo — more likely a walkman if you've just shelled out on a cymbal — is the sound of the cymbal having been processed, EQ'd, changed, for heaven's sake! So it isn't going to sound like the one I just got home. And my bedroom is hardly acoustically perfect.

It's apparent that there's a gap between the bedroom-based little league and the big league that is Grand Canyonesque. Big hitter Simon Phillips remarked that he couldn't feel confident playing a kit until he could hear it coming back through a monitor — wow! he's playing a different

instrument altogether. Most of the gigs I play are purely acoustic, the volume we play at not requiring big PA-age. So playing through a PA recently at the Powerhaus had me dazed and confused. The kit in my room is one instrument, its constituent parts related to one another, all ringing in sympathy, rather than eleven separate instruments each requiring their own EQ channels and gates (or if you're unlucky, only the bass and snare getting the treatment). Imagine telling a guitarist that he can only have two strings tonight. The whole process of recording music has stepped in and altered drums and drumming by a process of stealth; how many drum kits have you sat down and played that had stereo separation (electronics people, stay out of this!)? An example of how this has affected music is the difference between the grainy, vital rhythm tracks of old style Motown and the sterile, super-produced syrup that passes for soul these days. We know which works better, so what's going on? Maybe we should just shut up, set up, and get on with it.

It's doubtful that there's an answer. In fact I'm so confused I'm not even sure what the question was. But I do live in hope that there's a ride cymbal out there for me. There was a lovely one at this tatty old rehearsal room the other day, no badge, nothing, had such character, such warmth. But if I ever got to take it home, well maybe that'd be another story all together.

# chapter 2
## Tools Of The Trade

### Beatable Bargains

So... you're no longer smashing up the best G-Plan with knitting needles and chopsticks. The sound of furious jungle rhythms pounded out on cling-film covered biscuit tins has long since lost its primeval appeal. And 'Give It Away' transposed for breadboard, pan lid and Tupperware bacon storer just doesn't turn you on like it used to.

You're convinced it's time to cast off childish things (and talking of casting off, mum wants the knitting needles back anyway). Time to commit something a bit more serious. Something without which, deep down, you feel your claim to the title Drummer is empty and meaningless. The things they call A Drum Kit.

But where to start? Of course, you've read that your hero, Chuck Heavy, recommends King Kong extra deeps (custom Chameleon finish) mounted on Empire State triple-braced hardware and complemented by 30" Godzilla lead crashes. Unfortunately, you've checked out the prices down your local drum store and discovered you can't possibly afford even the not-so-very-deeps. Nor indeed can you

afford any other sparkling five-piece in the shop. You've considered moderating your ambitions, but quite frankly, "Hello, I'm a cowbeller!" just isn't you.

Still, your dad knows this geezer who used to be in the Whistling Hog Skiffle Kings, but who's now selling his kit because the wife wants the space in the garage for a freezer. It hasn't been played for twenty years, cymbal stands seem to be made of tent poles, and, judging by the smell, the heads from Algerian handbag leather. But he's only asking the hundred quid it took as many paper rounds to raise. Is it worth taking the gamble just so you can give a definite "Yes" to the mate who has asked you to join his band? Will other drummers laugh at you because it's got the manufacturers name all over the bass drum head? And who was this Plonka drum company anyway?

If you're short of cash, buying drums and percussion second-hand seems, on the face of it, like a sensible idea. Not only do you make a considerable saving on the retail price of equivalent new gear (although the better or rarer drums do tend to hold their value amazingly well), you often get a whole load of useful extras thrown in to boot — stools, cases, cymbals

✪ Ajax kit

✪ Duplex

✪ Melanie fantoms

and clamps. And there's no shortage of used gear around (you can see that just by looking in the back pages of Rhythm).

Whether you want a simple snare and stand for practising the rudiments, or a vast ten-piece double kick outfit with integral smoke machine — someone, somewhere is trying to get rid of one.

However, if you've just joined the great rhythmic brotherhood, then all this choice can be a bit bewildering. It's bad enough trying to buy a new kit, what with all the options that each manufacturer seems to offer — BMX this, KGB that, 3000 series hardware with the RKO finish and so on. However, look through the second-hand ads and you'll discover a whole forgotten world of names and model numbers. Just what is a Hayman Vibrasonic? Or a Trixon 'Conical' kit? Or a Melanie Fantom? It's hard enough to know what's worth ringing up about, let alone parting with the dosh for. No wonder the only alternative seems to be to rush out and buy the £299 Taiwanese budget job that got the good review the other month. And of course, that what reviews in drum magazines are for, to guide you through the maze of new gear and help you get the best value for money. But who's going to advise you on the pile of wood and chrome which Mr Bloggs tells you once boomed out proud from behind the Whistling Hogs in their finest hour? Fortunately, you don't have to be the Arthur Negus of percussion to make a sensible decision about whether or not to buy. What you do need to know is how to test the gear for structural soundness; what bits, if any, might need replacing and how easy it would be to replace them. Because drums are relatively straightforward instruments, no one can pull the wool over your eyes and maintain that it's best investment opportunity since BP went private.

Naturally, when deciding how much a kit is worth, there are certain cases, such as extremely rare drums or particularly sought

after ones (Gretsch round badge kits, for example) where the price is as much determined by their past associations as their physical condition. I'll be looking at this aspect of the second-hand market, as well as giving more specific background detail on various defunct companies later, but for the moment we'll assume that all you're looking for is a kit to play on rather than be seen with.

When determining the general condition of a prospective purchase, the finish and the chrome work are pretty useful indicators, since they can tell you a lot about how the kit has been treated by its previous owners. If the exterior looks smart and well looked after, chances are that all the moving parts, such as they are, will be in good working order too. Don't get too hung up on cosmetic details, though. People spend a lot of time worrying about the finish, but really, this is the one thing which is easy to put right — usually with elbow grease and a dab of non-scratch liquid cleaner. If the covering is badly damaged, or simply not to your taste, then there are drum shops who will recover a kit for a reasonable sum. DIY packs, in a variety of colours, are also available from Remo. Don't be too hasty to follow fashion and recover everything black, since finishes such as sparkle and pearl, which a few years ago were considered somewhat vulgar, have made a big comeback.

As far as chrome work goes, don't be put off by small spots of rust. Again, elbow grease can work wonders; stage lighting, miracles. Extensive rusting is a problem though, particularly on rims as these are difficult and fairly expensive parts of the kit to replace, especially on older drums. Rusted chrome can also reveal that the kit has been stored for a long time in damp conditions, in which case the shells might well be warped or even rotten. Check them to see whether they (and rims) are perfectly round. This is a sensible precaution since shells can also get distorted in other ways. For example, thinner bass drum shells on older jazz kits, which have had double tom holders added at a later stage, can sometimes get squashed out of shape by the weight of the new holder and extra tom. And even if the shells seem perfectly okay from the outside, you should always check them inside for any sign of cracking or splitting. Remove heads if you need to. Poking about inside can also tell you a bit more about the history of the kit, or whether indeed the drums are all originally the same make. Extraneous drill holes can also reveal that hardware has been replaced or added at various times.

If there are going to be any problems, you'll usually find them in the hardware department — a fact, incidentally, which applies as much to new kits as to old. First of all, check that all the necessary bits and pieces are there, as tracking down the exact replacement part can be difficult and prove expensive. If the kit is presented to you as a large heap on the floor, you should set it up and, ideally, play it. This will not only give you a pretty good idea as to whether all the component parts fit together (and remain fitted together) as they should, but also reveal whether the kit is suitable for you. This may seem an obvious point, but on older kits where tom holders are fairly rudimentary and cymbal stands a bit on the short side, you can find that not everything ends up being positioned in the right place.

Nuts and bolts are the areas on which to concentrate. Check primarily for stripped threads on any of the locking bolts, particularly on cymbal and tom stands which have to support the considerable force of the enthusiast's stroke. It's especially important on stands where the rods screw directly onto the inner extension tube, rather than tightening around a nylon bush — the far more effective modern approach to securing

telescopic stands. Otherwise, you might find yourself experiencing the Titanic Phenomenon — cymbals and drums sinking gracefully to the floor while the band plays on. However, even if the stands do seem a little dodgy, don't despair. Extra insurance can be provided by fitting memory locks (or, cheaper and easier to find, hose clips) around the bits most likely to slip. Certainly, don't be put off by the fact that older stands and holders appear incredibly flimsy when compared to the chunky monsters of today. If you've seen Keith Moon in action on the Premier kits of yesteryear, you know that they are capable of taking quite a beating, providing, of course, they're fastened up tight.

In the best of all possible worlds it would also be worth checking the threads of all the nutboxes and tuning bolts too, just to make sure they're in good working order. If there is any damage, it's going to be impossible to tension heads evenly, and the drum will inevitably sound naff. However, many drum shops (particularly those specialising in second-hand gear) should be able to supply you with nutboxes and bolts or replace them for you, though for more obscure makes, you might well have to wait while they track the matching part down.

Pedals are another crucial area to check moving parts. On bass pedals, the weak points are the bolt which holds the beater in place and the clamp mechanism which holds the pedal to the bass drum hoop. Remember though that broken straps and springs can be replaced quite easily. Also remember when you try pedals out, that what at first appears to be a deficiency in their design or construction can usually be remedied by a quick squirt of WD-40, adjustment of the tension spring, or even, dare I say it, learning the correct pedal technique. However, you may find that some hi-hat stands, while supporting the old Kranki Jazz Lights perfectly adequately, just can't handle the considerable weight of a decent pair. If the rest of the kit seems sound enough, the best thing is to consider investing in a better hi-hat and/or bass drum pedal. While I don't believe that having the best drums will make you play any better or learn any faster, decent pedals will most definitely get you off on the right foot (and, of course, the left).

Another investment that may well prove worthwhile is a new set of heads. If the existing ones have deeply pitted surfaces or are extremely dirty or dusty, they're due for replacement anyway. But even if the heads seem in good condition, choosing another type of head might suit the drums and your playing style a lot better.

Shelling out another 30 or 40 quid for a complete set of new heads may seem rather stupid when the whole idea of buying second-hand was to save money, but even if you bought new, you'd have to accept whatever heads the manufacturer offered as part of the package. These too might prove to be the wrong type, in which case you've got the expense of replacement anyway. And of course, if you're anxious to make an impression, you can always cheat a bit by fitting a head with the name of a more prestigious drum manufacturer to the front of your bass drum. But remember, if you're buying a kit, don't fall for the same trick — look for the name on the drums as well.

Continuing our search for beatable bargains, let's now take a closer look at the various sectors of the 'second' market: budget, connoisseur and nearly new.

Concentrating on the ads with the smallest numbers after the pound sign, we find ourselves faced with a choice between the tried and trusted budget lines (such as Thunder, Hohner et al) or a whole load of manufacturers that many might have never heard of — not surprising really, considering most of them went out of production years ago. This latter group

includes such brands as Ajax, Beverley, Besson, Carlton, Hayman, Olympic and Trixon. While the temptation might be to plump for the devils you know, when it comes to value for money, it's the second lot which can often prove the better investment, providing you know what you're looking for.

For your general information, that second list of names all hail from the Sixties and early Seventies, the heyday of British drum manufacturing, certainly in terms of quantity, though some dispute the overall quality. At that time, entrepreneurial activity in the instrument world was fuelled by the great 'Beat Boom'. Basically, along came the Fab Four and suddenly everyone wanted to grow their hair and noses long, pick up a guitar or a pair of sticks and form a band. Immediately there was a demand for budget gear. On the drum front — the batter head, if you will — established companies like Ajax and Premier really took off, while others, like Boosey and Hawkes, better known for kitting out the Brighouse and Raistricks of this world, quickly decided to move into drum manufacture as well. The result was something like the mass Taiwanese invasion of the last few years — a whole host of British drum kits, all of which were virtually identical apart from the shape of the nutboxes or certain peculiarities in the design of the bass spurs.

But don't get the impression that cheap meant nasty. Although suffering from rather flimsy hardware (as indeed is the case with all drum kits made before circa '76), the drum shells on all these kits were generally manufactured to a high standard using traditional methods. Like many of the more expensive kits, the shells were quite thin, often only four ply, but were strengthened top and bottom by 'glue rings' — these being strips of thicker ply wood about one inch wide and a quarter of an inch deep. (Indeed, companies such as Drum Workshop and Premier still manufacture some of their drums with glue rings, although most other companies have dropped the glue rings, the strength of the drum coming from thicker shells.)

It's precisely because the shells are thin that these drums can sound extremely good, even though nigh on twenty years old. In fact, legend has it that Bill Bruford used an Olympic bass and toms for all his studio work with Yes and King Crimson — albeit stripped of their original covering and with hardware and hoops replaced by modern fittings. But for this very reason, when looking at a kit of this vintage, it's always advisable to make sure the shells are perfectly round and, in particular, that the bass drum hasn't been squashed out of shape, as can happen if too much weight has been put on it.

In general, you'll find bass drums and toms make a pretty good sound, even though the dimensions of the drums are quite small when compared to the extra deep cylinders of today. As always, decent heads help — in fact, the original heads were pretty naff and did nothing to make the drums sound more expensive than they were. Of all modern day designs, CS heads seem to work best on concert toms, making them ring out loud and clear, even if the shells are quite shallow. Incidentally, the sound can also be much improved by varnishing the inside of the shells.

Snare drums tend to be more problematic. Often the snare bed doesn't seem to be cut quite right, so it's impossible to get rid of extraneous buzzings. It also seems more difficult to get a real 'crack' out of the snares, but this is more to do with the fact that almost all of them have wooden shells. However, as the choice of snare drums is a very personal matter anyway, you can always spend time looking for that perfect backbeat at a later stage. Or, if you really do prefer a metallic sound over the wooden, then go for a Taiwanese chromed steel job, most of

which are perfectly good when tuned carefully.

Of course, apart from hardware, the greatest limitation with these older outfits is the size and number of drums per kit, since many Sixties' kits are 'modelled' on Fifties four-piece jazz setups. But having said that, five-piece kits with double-headed toms are fairly common, as are power sizes. But one thing to watch out for is that the drum isn't so old that it has pre-international head sizes, because, although heads are still available (Remo make them to order, for example), the choice is rather limited.

With a couple of exceptions, most of the names I've mentioned so far are pretty much of a muchness, so choosing between them really comes down to just how much stuff you're getting as part of the deal, whether you like the colour, and, of course, if all the pieces are still functioning. As I say, the main drawback is the hardware (particularly bass drum spurs and tom holders), which is often of such bad design that you might have to consider replacing it whatever its condition.

If you want something a little out of the ordinary, there are some Trixon kits floating about which have strangely shaped bass drums. For example, the front head of the 'Conical' kit's bass drum is several inches smaller in diameter than the batter head, while on another kit (sometimes referred to as 'Egg-shaped') the bass drum is oval. These 'innovations' seem to have been introduced purely for novelty's sake — no mystical acoustic science at work here — and the other drums in the kit were constructed as normal. But since Trixon seemed also to specialise in garish sparkle finishes (the mustard hue is my favourite), they are well worth tracking down if your taste errs towards the eccentric.

Hayman is another name which stands out from the crowd, not just because they feature unusual round nutboxes (later

⊙ **Ludwig Black Beauty**

adopted by the American manufacturers Camco and then Drum Workshop). Look inside the drums and you could find the famous Vibrasonic lining, a spray coating of a special material which helps give the drums much more power and projection.

Vibrasonic drums were launched in 1968 and proved extremely popular throughout the early Seventies. Although the company later went bust, the name was revived for a while about ten years ago, although the kits in question, while sporting that distinctive circular nutbox and round Hayman badge, originated in Taiwan.

Although later associated with products emanating from the US (in the late Eighties a range of cymbals imported by Arbiters, for example), the name Rogers was also to be found on British made drums during this period. Like Hayman, they had an excellent reputation among professional players, so add them to your list of possibilities.

Let's now cast the beadies across the Great Water and have a look at the second-hand market for kits of US origin — particularly Gretsch, Ludwig and Slingerland.

This is very much a different world — what you might call the 'classic vintage' market. Kits and individual drums are much more expensive, but resale values remain higher too. It's all to do with the fact that, until the Japanese began their export drive towards world domination at the end of the Seventies, it was the American kits which were regarded as the real prestige models — the drums that many drummers aspired to, but few could afford to choose.

Apart from cost (high import duties) and the fact that they were difficult to get hold of (poor British distribution and marketing), their laurels were woven from the reputations of the first generation of drumming 'influences'. Great men like Art Blakey, Max Roach and Tony Williams were synonymous with Gretsch, Buddy Rich with Slingerland, Joe Morello with Ludwig. Also, perhaps more so than with British drums, it seemed that each of these makes definitely did have a specific character (and, indeed, they still do). Gretsch drums tend to be warm and rather thuddy, with very little overtone — the sound being due, like the Hayman Vibrasonics, to a special coating on the inside of the shell which soaks up most of the internal vibrations. Ludwig drums on the other hand were quite the reverse — really big and open, with loadsa overtones. No wonder they emerged as firm favourites with Seventies power rockers like John Bonham and Ginger Baker, who needed to boom out across the ever-increasing megawatts of guitar amplification. Slingerland were different again — much more high pitched and ringy, with an almost latin sound to the toms (which is no doubt why they were favoured by players like Airto Moreira).

If you're looking for a classic sound with a lot of historical association and just a teensy-weensy bit of snob value, then these makes might be for you, particularly as the represent as much a financial as a musical investment.

The Gretsch kits to be seen with are the earlier ones with the round as opposed to the octagonal badges adopted in the later years. However, they are extremely rare and consequently expensive. Vintage second-hand Ludwigs are also distinguished by different badges — the pre-'68/69 ones having a small gold 'crown' badge, for example. However, the important changes in Ludwig kits actually occurred in the early Seventies, when they stopped constructing their shells from a three ply roll of mahogany with glue rings and instead, began to die-mould them from six plies of maple/mahogany combination. Though the switch in manufacturing process meant that the shells on these later kits are more likely to be perfectly round, that classic Ludwig sound belongs in fact to the older drums.

Among drummers of some experience, Ludwig snares have always commanded a considerable amount of respect in their own right. The classic classic is undoubtedly the brass-shelled Black Beauty, which used to be available in two options: Superphonic or Supersensitive — the latter featuring individually tensionable snare wires. Another favourite is the steel shelled 400 Superphonic, the model that was invariably to be found between Ringo's knees. (On the subject of recommended snares, another one closer to home is the Premier 2000.)

If you're looking for visual variations a la Trixon, Ludwig happily oblige in the form of their Vistalite and Staccato kits.

Vistalite kits are in fact made out of perspex and date from the early/mid-Seventies, when bands like Curved Air (Stewart Copeland's old back-seat haunt) had all their instruments made out of perspex. Rumour has it that Ludwig endorsee Ginger Baker started the trend by bending his own sheets of perspex in front of the gas fire. Ludwig then offered to make a better job of it and thus Vistalite was born. Like platform shoes and flares, they proved

to be one of those phases which everyone seemed to go through, and no doubt they'll be due for a comeback pretty soon. People who still confess to owning these kits rate them pretty highly, especially the snares.

The drumming equivalent of bell bottoms was undoubtedly the Staccato kits. These were made of fibreglass and featured extra-deep shells which bent and flared slightly at the bottom — the idea being that they would project sound more towards the audience than onto the drum riser. A more extreme application of this philosophy was marketed by another American company, North, whose drums looked very much like those small bent funnels you see on ships.

Although American drums are extremely well made and thoroughly deserve their reputation, it wasn't until the late Eighties that their hardware was brought up to the standard of their Japanese rivals.

It was Tama who were responsible for producing the first really substantial pieces of hardware, and so it's not surprising that in the early Eighties you find a lot of rock drummers rallying to their banner. Incidentally, they were originally marketed under the name Star (hence later on, Artstar, Granstar, Star Classic etc.), and they also produced a budget range (similar to Pearl's Maxwin) called Hoshino, which is well worth investigating for the quality of the hardware alone.

Another Japanese manufacturer to look out for is Trak. No longer imported into this country after they failed to break into the monopoly held at the time by Pearl and Yamaha, they were nevertheless excellent drums, particularly the mid-priced 200 range.

I suspect that, having been thoroughly bamboozled by all this information, most people would quite happily plump for a kit that they already knew something about. In other words, 'nearly new' gear which is

**✪ A Staccato kit**

either still in production or has just been superseded by 'this year's model' and as a consequence, still has plenty of information available on it in the form of catalogues and perhaps even reviews in back issues of drum magazines. There's no need, then, for me to go into great detail here, nor for me to get into a fruitless discussion about just who is the best drum manufacturer of them all. I'd rather save my breath for really pertinent discussions, like who's the world's most brilliant drum roadie...

In many ways this is the safest way to go about hunting down a second-hand kit, since specifications are already known, reputations established, and should there be any problems, you can go direct to the maker or distributor for spare or extra parts. Since it's easy to find out how much the gear cost in the first place, you are also best able to judge whether the asking price really is a fair one. But since the seller is likely to know that as well, don't expect any great bargains. A shiny Pearl Masters at 50 quid below its RRP could still be several hundred quid above the DPP (Desired Purchase Price).

Even if a kit appears untouched by human hand (well, most drummers are animals, aren't they?), do still give it a thorough going over in the manner described above.

Which brings me round to the epilogue of this saga of rhythm on the cheap — buying second-hand cymbals.

The good news here is that, like drum kits, checking a cymbal's physical condition is a relatively simple matter. The main thing to look for is any sign of splitting. This occurs most often around the outer edge or the bell, where in either case the cracks will run across the grooves. Less common are cracks which start in the grooves on the surface of the cymbal round the bell area. Indeed, it's not unknown for a split of the second type to follow a groove right the way round, leaving you with a cymbal of much reduced diameter. I'm told you can get some interesting sounds that way.

Obviously you can't fail to notice the really big cracks, but very occasionally, cymbals have hairline fractures or other faults in the metal which are virtually undetectable and will only reveal themselves by metamorphosing into faults of a more serious kind later on.

Quite frankly, there's absolutely nothing you can do about this, it's a risk you take even with brand new cymbals. Indeed, as most long-in-the-tooth pros have experienced at some time or other, even brand new, top quality cymbals can shatter on their first gig for no apparent reason whatsoever. The difference is, of course, they won't need to part with a whole year's beer money to buy a replacement.

So, the golden rule here is, if you can't see it, there's really no point in worrying about it. But remember, don't tighten up the wing nuts on your cymbal stands so much that there's no lateral movement. Even if

there are no cracks to start with, believe me, there soon will be.

Dirty cymbals respond well to elbow grease, especially when applied in conjunction with any of the several proprietary cymbal cleaners on the market (no Brillo Pads, please). Cymbals do need to be kept clean, since if the corrosion is allowed to build up, their sound becomes as dead as the finish. Ideally, you should always wear gloves to handle them (no kidding), since the sweat from your fingers makes a highly efficient corrosive agent.

Apart from the points mentioned, there's very little else to concern yourself with, apart from whether or not you like the sound. In the best of all possible worlds, you should get someone else to play them to you, preferably with the kit, so you can hear what they sound like from out front. And if you're adding to your collection, ideally, you should bring your other ones along to see what they all sound like en masse, particularly when you're mixing different makes together (not a cardinal sin as the cymbal companies would have us believe).

Incidentally, if you're worried that someone might be trying to pass off an Everthin Tinkly as something more expensive, never fear. Most cymbals have the manufacturer's name stamped into the metal as well as printed on the surface; so even if the ink has rubbed off, indelible evidence is to be found elsewhere.

Before you go and look at gear of any sort, do find out as much as you can over the phone, to avoid a wasted trip. I remember ringing up about some cymbals advertised as 'Six months old... never gigged', and in his enthusiasm to get rid of them, the voice on the other end said, "Oh, they're great... been giving them some real welly over these last three years, yet on stage they look as though they'd been made only yesterday."

Happy hunting.

# A Gut Feeling

Modern drummers seem to have a problem with their snares: achieving a clean, playable sound without intrusive rattles and buzzes seems depressingly out of reach. There are many supposed solutions: complex adjustable mechanisms, the use of straps, and different materials for the snares themselves — coiled wire, nylon, guitar-string-like composites, and even aircraft cable. The problem is that the material needs to be elastic enough to follow the contours of hoop and head under minimum tension, yet hard enough to give a clear, bright response, but not so dense that an inappropriate amount of energy will be required to move it. Unfortunately, no such material exists. However, the ideal solution is found in bypassing one of these requirements: elasticity. So instead of using an elastic material that will conform to any convex surface, the trick is to use a non-elastic that is persuaded to adopt only the required shape.

This material is sheep gut (dedicated vegetarians need read no further!), and nowadays comes mostly from Australia and Pakistan. It is made from long strips of wet gut that are twisted to form a cylinder and allowed to dry. The resultant 'cord' is then sometimes polished smooth. It is often weatherproofed as well, but since this version cannot be soaked to make it pliable, it isn't suitable for out purpose.

The setting process is similar to lapping calf heads, in that the gut is soaked and allowed to dry that way. The difference is that a head dries under tension, thus being forced into shape, while gut must dry under almost no tension, so as not to unwind it, and also because that is how it will be used. If done properly, you will have snares of light, fairly hard material which will follow the contour of the bottom of the drum under very little tension — the ideal snare material.

Because the gut is in continuous contact with the head, it has a damping action. Under low tension, it will rise from the head very easily for a playing stroke, but discourages the vibration of the drum head, thus controlling excess buzzing such as is caused by sympathetic vibration with other instruments. Also, since it rises so easily for a valid stroke, the drum is allowed for that moment to resound more fully than with the less consistent rise of other materials, giving simultaneously a fuller and clearer sound. The sound is brighter than with wire snares, which means the effective volume and projection become greater and the sound is characteristically very dry.

However, one problem arises here.

As I said, the snares should be at the minimum possible tension for a clean response; if not, the drum responds less well to a soft stroke than one equipped with wire snares, although at the correct tensions it is just as responsive. Also, the brightness decreases at an earlier point with increased tension. Essentially, though, this is a matter of learning to use lower tensions rather than an inherent drawback. At correct tension, the drum is not only as responsive as (and brighter than) a wire snare drum, but has a much less choked sound. However, the lower tension can lead to a problem with sloppy strainers since there is not as much tension to keep them in place. Even so, nobody I know finds this a serious problem, and with the very low tension the snares seem to last indefinitely. I know of one very loud player who has been using the same set of snares for three or four years now, and they show no sign of age.

The real drawback with gut snares is the difficulty of fitting. It is a fairly skilled job, and takes three days or so to allow the gut to dry completely. Changing the snare head can be problematic, but for myself, when fitting gut to a drum, I incorporate a removable bracket on one side of the drum, so the snares can be detached and re-fitted on that side without losing their configuration, thus allowing heads to be removed and replaced. With some drums, particularly those with small snare gates and strainers with little 'throw', the snares cannot easily be thrown away from the drum. Most players find this loss outweighed by the gains, and remember, you don't have to throw the snares off to prevent buzzing — it isn't there anyway. Another potential problem is change in tension with atmospheric humidity; in practice I find this small, and since I always use the same gut length for all the snares of one drum, any change is pretty constant across the snares and rarely enough to cause any real worries.

The last problem is the worst of all: gut snares are too clean for some players. Every player will tell you that he or she wants as clean a snare sound as possible. In practice, some don't, and I suspect that many don't like the way it shows up shortcomings in their technique! However, practising on a gut drum does sharpen up your playing — sometimes considerably.

And engineers love them! In general, my approach to the drum set (treating it as a complete instrument, with its resonances contributing to a complete and unified tonal quality) does not impress engineers who simply want to control everything separately. But they do appreciate the brightness, clean, consistent sound and lack of buzz. I have been told of engineers asking drummers to put the snares on a gut drum during a level check, and refusing to believe they already are on.

Gut snares are quite a mental turnaround for some, but worth considering. Some of the players who do use gut preferentially are Steve White, Harbans Srih, and the redoubtable Johanne James (formerly the drummer with

Freehand). Steve and Harbans are both players who are finding that the depth of their involvement with their music is demanding more than modern instruments and technology can supply, and as for Johanne — if you've heard his playing, you'll know what I mean.

So that's it. You can't buy gut snares in shops, and it is a very old-fashioned idea; the earliest snare drums had gut snares, and when alternative materials came along, manufacturers couldn't wait to change. But studio requirements have made their unusual clarity of sound and brightness, coupled with no lack of response, once more a very viable proposition.

## One In The Hand

The wide and wonderful world of percussion encompasses everything from timpani and tubular bells, to tambourines and triangles. Here, we're going to look at some of the more common or garden hand-held species.

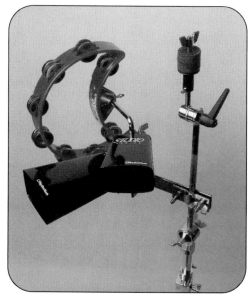

✪ **Tambourine and cowbells**

○ **Meinl percussion: cow bells, caxixi, claves . . .**

Apart from their relative cheapness (compared, for example, to a 22 tom, double bass drum setup), one of the attractions must surely be that they don't require years of patient practice or a trip to the Andes to learn how to get a decent sound out of. In addition, while they give any drummer the possibility of adding extra sounds to a conventional kit, they're also very useful in the recording studio, or for singers who don't know what to do with themselves during those fifteen minute instrumental breaks.

So, in no particular order, here is a brief history and description of a few types and their variations.

### AFUCHÉ/CABASA

In its native environment, the afuché/cabasa consists of a clay gourd with beads threaded on string or netting around its circumference. The instrument can be shaken, twisted or turned in the palm of the hand, to make the beads rub across the surface of the clay. Be warned though: if you do want to go for that ethnic authenticity, these instruments are very fragile. A good compromise though, is the tekke gourd shaker, which combines the shape of the original with the strength of fibreglass construction.

The modern cabasa works on much the same principle, although this time, linked ball-bearings are rubbed across a ribbed stainless steel cylinder. Obviously, this gives it a much sharper, metallic sound — something akin to several hundred crickets clearing their throats in unison.

The only 'maintenance' that this instrument might require is as a result of over-enthusiastic use. As the groove hots up and your palms get sweaty, salt does tend to corrode the balls — and that wouldn't do, would it? And — carrying on in the spirit of the great British double entendre — the best thing is to give everything a good wipe down after use, in much the same way as a good guitarist cleans his string.

## VIBRA-SLAP

The vibra-slap is a modern derivation of an instrument originally fashioned from the mandibulae of such perissodactyl mammals as the equus asinus, the equus hemionus, and the agile and bovine genus capra... In other words, the jaw-bones of asses, donkeys or goats.

Back in ancient times, once you had managed to extract the jaw of whichever of these animals happened to be to hand (a difficult task if the creature was still alive), you then struck the bone to produce a pleasing rattle from the loose teeth.

Nowadays, the onward march of civilisation has refined that idea into a boot-shaped piece of sprung steel with a wooden ball at one end and a sound chamber at the other. This chamber contains several rivets set on a piece of metal. When the ball is struck, the rivets vibrate against the walls of

❂ **Extra percussion to the hi-hat**

the sound box to produce a sound not unlike that of a pneumatic woodpecker. Latin Percussion also produce a slightly more advanced version, described (somewhat unimaginatively) as the Vibra-slap II. This allows you to expand the range of sounds through several interchangeable chambers — a metal one with steel rivets, and two wooden ones, each with a slightly different tone. Add to this a clip-on tambourine jingle (for that subtle 'ching' effect), and you've got an instrument which any perissodactyl would be envious of.

## COWBELL

Another instrument which owes much to bovine influences, is the cowbell, originally to be found around the necks of Swiss cows. Unfortunately, the cows proved unable to grip the sticks for any length of time, and eventually the cowherds took to playing the cowbells themselves.

Nowadays, cowbells are to be found in just about every form of music from funk to classical, and if you want to add one to your existing setup, there are a variety of prices and sizes to choose from. It is recommended that the larger cowbells should be hand-held, and it's possible to get an interesting range of tones by dampening the bell with one hand and striking it in different places. If, however, you're using it with a drum kit, the normal thing is to mount it on the bass drum hoop via a post and clamp. If this is uncomfortable, or if you just don't want to mark that nice, shiny hoop, you can always look at the post which Premier make for drum corps. This allows the cowbell to be mounted on a tom by being screwed down beneath the most convenient tension rod. The only disadvantage is that, with the mount in place, it might be difficult to get in its case, and, of course, it's likely to cock up your efforts to tune the drum.

### AGOGO

Not to be confused with a go-go dancer (a scantily clad nightclub gyrator) or the French term a gogo ('as much as you like'), the agogo is in fact a piece of hand-held percussion which looks (and sounds) very like two miniature cowbells, one at each end of a piece of bent metal. As one agogo is larger than the other, it follows that they are of different pitches, and this allows many complicated rhythms to be built up.

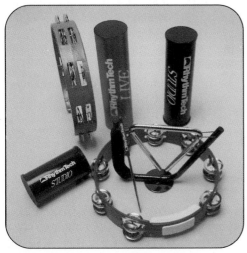

○ **Rhythm Tech shake, rattle and roll**

The ones you're most likely to see around are those made by LP, but if you can find either the Gope Brazilian version or the cruder looking African ones, you'll find that these have a more interesting tone, and their springier steel joint allows them to be 'clanged' together.

The idea behind wooden agogos is much the same, but the finished product is really no more than a couple of light duty wooden blocks on a stick with a grooved part which can be scraped rather like a guiro.

### MARACAS

Maracas and, indeed, all other instruments that go 'rattle' in the night, are probably the most popular pieces of hand-held percussion, especially as it's possible to get your hands on a pair of plastic, multi-coloured shakos el cheapos for as little as a fiver. After that, you're limited only by what you can shake out of your wallet. For example, for about £50 you could be rattling a pair of LP Rawhide maracas, which will give you that deeper, richer and more authentic tone.

LP and Rhythm Tech also makes lots of other things you can shake, rattle and roll. In fact, of all, the Rhythm Tech shaker is probably the best buy — it's tubular, plastic and comes in various sizes.

When choosing a pair of maracas, the only advice I can really give you is to make sure that the 'shot' inside (the bits that do all the rattling) has plenty of weight, so as to make a nice 'chick' sound when it hits the sides of the container. But having said all that, I seem to remember Valerie Singleton on *Blue Peter*, showing us how to make a cracking set of maracas out of old squeezy washing-up liquid bottles, sticky-back plastic and half a pound of dried peas. Remember, though, if you're going to use scissors, make sure there's a grown-up there to show you how...

## GANZA AND CAXIXI

Apart from nuts, coffee and the victorious 1994 World Cup squad, Brazil has also given us the ganza and the caxixi. Of roughly similar spec', these instruments consist of a woven basket with a gourd bottom, in which are placed small pebbles or the like. Used as a shaker, you can get a lot of interesting sounds depending on whether the filler material strikes the basket or the harder gourd surface.

## TAMBOURINES

The etymologically inclined amongst you will be fascinated to learn that 'tambourine' is derived from the 16th Century Middle Flemish word tamborijn, meaning 'a small drum'.

In 20th Century England, as long as it has jingles, it's a tambourine. Otherwise it can be any colour, shape, size and material you like — from a circular wooden one with a tuneable single head, to a fluorescent green crescent-shaped affair.

## FLEXITONE

This is a metal frame with a sprung metal plate and two beaters (one either side) which vibrate against the plate, while the tone or pitch is controlled by bending the metal plate with the thumb. A difficult sound to describe in words, so I won't try; but a very unusual and original instrument... honest, guv.

## CLAVES

Two pieces of rosewood about six inches long which, when banged together, sound, not surprisingly, like two six inch pieces of rosewood being banged together. However, as Shakespeare might have said (but didn't), not all rosewoods smell so sweet...

Research has shown (and this is surprising) that some makes are actually louder than others, particularly those made by Sonor or John Hornby Skewes.

## SAMBA WHISTLE

A whistle with three holes which produces (can you guess?) three different tones — which must make it three times as annoying.

## TRIANGLE

I won't insult anybody's intelligence by telling you what these look like, but if you can imagine a three-sided...

Although constantly derided for its apparent simplicity, the triangle is actually a very tricky instrument to play well. Various finger-damping techniques are used to create sounds both funky and artistically 'acceptable'.

Look out for the Suzuki brand name, which is supplied by Boosey & Hawkes.

## GUIRO

Also known as a 'torpedo', these glorified scrapers come in a variety of materials, including fibreglass, bamboo, wood, metal and gourd. The wooden models can be hit in much the same way as the woodblock.

And that just about concludes our trip around the world of hand-held percussion. The more resourceful amongst you might like to make your own bits and pieces out of things like beer cans, household containers, coconut shells, bits of the garden gate etc.. Toy shops can also turn up some interesting items in the shape of small cymbals, bells, shakers and scrapers.

# The Big Break

For some crazy reason it seems to have become macho to break cymbals. Maybe it's a sign of the times, but I heard a story recently of a father who went into a drum shop to buy a cymbal for his teenage son and more or less bragged that nothing would stand up to his son's aggressive playing, he breaks everything. Sure enough a couple of weeks later he was back with a smile on his face and the now broken cymbal, boasting that he'd told the guys in the shop nothing would stand up to his son's playing and demanding a replacement. The father had two chances — and the first was no chance. So, he'd wasted his bread.

As a former drum shop owner, I saw a great many broken cymbals. Some were damaged around the bell or the mounting hole, while others had cracks at right angles to the edge; I once even owned a completely inverted ride cymbal which had unfortunately been in a car crash. In my time I've heard the most amazing excuses for why and how these cymbals became knackered. It's hardly surprising that no one ever admitted they'd hit their instrument wrongly or abused it. And any retailer worth his salt knows how to run his fingers around the very edge of a cymbal to ascertain exactly where it's been abused. (There's almost always an abrasion in the edge nearest to the crack.) If he feels you have a genuine case, he'll pass your problem onto the manufacturer who will in turn want to know some basic facts about the life it's lead. He'll want to know the type of music its owner is involved in; is it heavy metal, rock, jazz or pop? How big are the venues it's been played in? Has it been miked up, or has it been vainly trying to keep up with banks of Marshall 4x12"s? Does the cymbal's owner personally set up his equipment, or does he leave it to the tender ministrations of an ex-window cleaner?

But I digress. The guy examining what is rapidly becoming your expensive problem, will also be very interested in how it's transported. Does it have a soft bag, a fibre case, or better still its own moulded Cymbal Safe? Or does it simply sit with the other cymbals on top of the bass drum in its case? What happens to the case/bag after it's packed? Is it thrown into the back of a truck and wedged into a 'safe' position by the spare wheel? Is it the last thing to go into the van, thereby being the first to fall out onto the ground when the doors are opened? Is it carefully laid on top of the rest of the gear? If so, how far can the bag slide, and what's in its way when the driver makes an emergency stop? (A typical bag-full of uncontrolled cymbals, weighing about 10 kilos, would make quite a mess of anyone's hair-do if it came in their direction.)

So, having weighed up all these factors, the manufacturer will come to a decision about replacement — one which is often based on keeping the dealer happy. That said, the amount of returns the makers get is less than one in 500, so they're hardly inundated.

So let's get it straight: besides it being un-cool to break cymbals, it's inconvenient and always expensive. In all my years, I've seen very few cymbals that were genuinely damaged because of a manufacturing fault. Besides being accidentally dropped (which you are able to insure against), breakage is invariably the end result of ignorance (or perhaps it would be more diplomatic to say lack of education). And the manufacturers are convinced far more cymbals are damaged in transit, set-up and tear-down than when they're being played, even with a high degree of ferocity. Therefore, for your un-education, here are some of the best ways to break cymbals.

**1.** *Do screw the wing-nut on the cymbal tilter down on the cymbal as tightly as possible; don't give it room to move or breathe on the spigot.*

**2.** *Make sure the threaded spigot at the top of the cymbal stand has no plastic sleeve, thus ensuring constant metal-to-metal contact, ultimately resulting in an attractive 'key-hole' effect being filed into the centre hole.*

**3.** *Throw away the felt washers at the top of the cymbal stand but keep the large metal one; this way the cymbal will have no shock suspension and, for a time, a most unusual tone.*

**4.** *Try to find a ratchet tilter which moves (or better still, loosen the wing-nut holding the tilter and cymbal steady) — with luck, you may find the tilter allowing the cymbal to spectacularly fall in an arc and smash against the cymbal stand.*

**5.** *Make sure there are two tripod legs facing towards the audience (just one would make it too stable); this way, if you really lay into your cymbal, it stands a better chance of falling frontways into the audience to achieve a never to be forgotten effect.*

**6.** *Don't crash the cymbal with a glancing sideways blow, or even whip the stick away as soon as it's struck. Hit it with a full-blooded blow right through the cymbal.*

**7.** *Set your hi-hat really high so you can seriously attack the edges of both top and bottom cymbals at the same time; and don't forget to clamp that top cymbal clutch as tightly as possible, so it puts pressure on the bell.*

**8.** *Cram as many cymbals as possible into the case; in extremis, put some the wrong way up, and ensure they're able to rub against one another constantly. If you have a fibre case, it's a good idea to have some sort of slit in the bottom so one (or, better still, two) cymbals are able to slip through slightly and scrape the ground.*

**9.** *Don't protect your cymbals in their case with foam, bubble-wrap or even a blanket; the idea of slipping a cymbal-hole sized plastic nut and bolt (or even an old hi-hat clutch) through all your cymbals to make sure that the smaller ones don't slip to the bottom as soon as you pick up the case, is too ridiculous to contemplate.*

**10.** *Finally, do buy the wrong cymbal for the job. The manufacturers' designations on their products are simply there to blind you with science. It's price that counts — why not use a paper-thin crash for your metal music if you want to; after all, the manufacturer is bound to replace it when it breaks.*

Seriously though, folks, this last commandment is possibly the most important. The reason the cymbal companies make heavy, medium, light and all the divisions in between, is because they want you to make the right choice for yourself and ultimately be satisfied and therefore happy with their product, whereupon you'll come back for more.

We spoke earlier about replacing faulty cymbals, but frankly, the major companies don't, by and large, make mistakes with their manufacturing processes — they can't afford to. Some twenty-five years ago, one famous cymbal company almost went out of business because of the amount of broken cymbals which were being returned to them. Ultimately the fault didn't lie in their product at all, it was simply in the guys playing them. It was a time when music and drummers were becoming more rocky and aggressive, while this particular concern's cymbals remained basically jazz-orientated instruments. So they beefed up their formula, educated the drummers, and the cymbals didn't come back anymore.

With cymbals, it's horses for courses and your music will dictate what weight of cymbal you need. If you break splash cymbals — and many people do — unless you're loaded, it's crazy to go out and buy another fast one for lots of money and wait for it to break again. Check out something like a small crash. Likewise, if you're thumping away every night in a rock band, while a heavy crash may not speak as quickly as you'd like, it will definitely last longer than a lightweight one and consequently save you money. Compromise — you know it makes sense.

I'll leave you with two thoughts. A cymbal is an instrument with thousands of years of history and expertise behind its manufacturing process, it's not by any means just a plate of metal. Even though many professionals get advantageous deals on cymbals, the manufacturers state that pros don't break them with anything like the same regularity as guys who don't play drums for a living.

## Love Thy Neighbour

Over the years, *Rhythm* has been inundated with enquiries from novice noiseniks seeking to soundproof their drum rooms and re-establish diplomatic relations with next door. It's not immediately clear whether these missives have come from drummers or their families, but I suspect it's the latter, because invariably it's the innocent bystander who suffers most from 'passive drumming'. After all, no serious drummer is likely to be unhappy about the racket he's making.

Let's face it though, drums are noisy and obtrusive instruments when played in the home environment, and unfortunately there's no easy way to treat a room in such a way that will prevent all the sound frequencies inherent in a drum kit from leaking out. What we're setting out to eliminate is the heaviness of the bass drum in the bottom end, the cymbals sizzling away at the very top, and the snare drum somewhere in the middle. In effect, a room

acts just like a speaker cabinet, where the bigger the enclosure, the more emphasised the bass end will be, so the major problem encountered when soundproofing is how to lose those highly audible bottom tones.

You can actually make a very good job of stopping the sound going sideways and we'll get to this later, but stopping it going up and down is more difficult — and correspondingly more expensive. (Recording studios have been known to spend bundles on floating floors on thick rubber so the sound doesn't escape.) Therefore, a garage, basement or ground floor room with nothing below is probably the best starting point if you wish to create a studio environment.

In the past musicians have stapled egg boxes to the walls of their spare rooms in an effort to kill the sound leakage. In fact, all this does is make the environment less attractive acoustically for themselves without really hindering the penetration of sound.

There's an obvious relationship between the thickness of the walls and the possibility of sound penetrating them; ie. you'd be hard pushed to hear drums being played behind a castle rampart. So what we have to do is artificially thicken our walls by creating an air cavity, and add filters which the sound will find hard to pass through. As I intimated, a bedroom in a house is not as simple to soundproof as a garage, because there are bound to be awkward windows and doors to be dealt with, and vertical leakage is a problem too. The 'air-sandwich' principle I'm about to outline will, with some ingenuity, work anywhere, but if you have the option, go for the garage or some other external structure — even a shed.

What we're doing with our soundproofing is breaking down sound waves by filtering them first through perforated sheets of hardboard, then mineral fibre slabs, an air gap, roofing felt, and finally the wall.

We begin by attaching 25mm horizontal battens at the very top of our walls, and fixing sheets of roofing felt (or old carpet) to them with large headed nails, thus creating a curtain and a 25mm air gap which the sound finds difficult to bridge. (You could cover your windows in the same way, but it'll make ventilation impossible and block off your emergency exit, so if you have the patience, make up removable frames for your windows of the 'air-sandwich' type. Failing that, thick carpet hung on hooks over the windows and doors work well enough.) Next, fit one 50mm batten to the floor and another to the ceiling 50mm away from the wall, and fix vertical struts 600mm apart to the back of these to support the mineral fibre slabs (Rockwell number 5). Then put the fibre slabs in place on the vertical struts, having cut them to size with a bread knife. You'll make a lot of unhealthy dust, so it's a very good idea to wear a mask, long-sleeved shirt and gloves. Then place more vertical slats to the outside of those floor and ceiling battens to hold the slabs in place.

Now you're ready to fit the pegboard. Cut it to size and fit to the top and bottom battens with your large headed nails, then use screws to secure the board down its long edges, having first ensured the vertical joins correspond with an upright. All dodgy joins can be tidied up later with, say, skirting board, architrave and ramin slats.

Right, that's your walls sorted; now to concentrate on the ceiling.

First, secure some more battens to the corners near the ceiling and stand by to nail up the pegboard. At the same time, slip some pre-cut fibre slabs into place in the substantial air gap between it and the ceiling. (If ever you needed a friend, it's now.) Finally, secure planed timber mouldings over the joins to make them look better and stop them sagging. Alternatively, if you're doing a bedroom, you could get into the loft and lay the fibreboard between the joists and achieve almost the same insulation. (Soundproofing works more efficiently if it doesn't actually touch the structure it's isolating.)

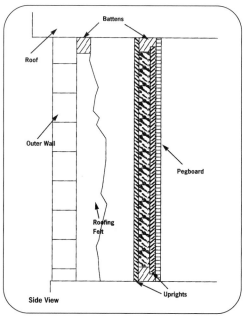

Wooden Batten     Outer Wall

Roofing Felt

Mineral Slab

Pegboard

**The Basic Principle**

Battens

Roof

Outer Wall

Pegboard

Roofing Felt

Uprights

**Side View**

✪ **Sound proofing: the basic principle**            ✪ **Side view**

If you've decided to soundproof an upstairs room rather than a garage, you're now going to have to get to grips with the floor. As I said, sound has an annoying habit of travelling downwards too, so you're going to have to float a new floor on something dense which will soak up the sound. The new floor can be made from interlocking chipboard laid on sturdy foam rubber, layers of thick carpet, Rockwool, or even newspaper. If you want to do the job properly, 2″ thick Rockwool is the business, but it's expensive whereas the other stuff isn't. By the way, if you're using newspaper, you'll need an extra inch of thickness all over, which could be a problem to accumulate besides being a fire risk (check with your local council.) At the edges you can either leave a small gap where the boards meet the wall to stop any sound transmission, or fit a rubber gasket all the way round.

Fortunately, there is a cheaper alternative involving much less upheaval. Simply make a raft from large, and ideally portable, pieces of 3/4″ shuttering plywood to sit the drum set on, and glue dense foam to the underside of it. It's obviously not as effective as treating the whole floor, but it will certainly isolate the bass drum's sound reasonably well.

We haven't said anything about doors yet, but here we have an option or two. If it's a bedroom, we can actually fit another door into the frame opening the other way to the original. Or if it's a cavity door, we can fill it with something. Drill a hole or two in the top and pour concrete (preferably) or sand in to really give it some mass. Or you could actually attach the same 'air-sandwich' structure I've detailed for the walls to your door.

If you've gone the garage route and have a side door for access, it's relatively easy to build a block wall as close to the front door as possible. It doesn't need footings because it won't be load-bearing and can always be knocked down when the drummer takes up a more socially acceptable hobby. Now you can treat that wall in exactly the same way as the others. If you don't have a side door, though, you're going to have to do a bit more work and lose some precious space inside by building a stud wall as close as possible to the door, and actually hanging a door in it. So, to get in you open the main door, and then the internal one. (If you've an 'up-and-over' door, you'll need to open it fully to ascertain where to construct your wall, but this will at least give you space to store your mountain bike and a few crates of beer. Remember to make the new door big enough to get your gear in and out in the unlikely case that all your practising results in your getting a gig. Now you can hang your roofing felt inside and build the rest of your 'air-sandwiched' wall as before.

Supposing you've an old-fashioned garage with double wooden doors which open outwards. No problem. Fix one door so it won't move, and use the other as the entrance. Then treat both as per the walls (having first painted inside any windows you may have, so it doesn't look messy from outside). Otherwise attach thick carpets to them.

The problem with making a room sound-tight is that you're creating a stuffy environment without ventilation. And while this may well be acceptable in the winter, in the summer it will be like a sauna — ideal for losing weight but otherwise unhealthy. You could get a couple of fans, but all they really do is stir the existing air up. What you need is air-conditioning of some sort. It's possible to fit ventilation to bring air from the outside world through the false ceiling you've constructed via flexible ducting tube, ending in a hole in the wall (or window) and a fan in the ceiling. But if you do this you'll need a sound attenuator (like an exhaust muffler) in the middle of the duct to stop the sound escaping through the piping. Otherwise you can practise till you can't stand any more, then throw open the door, gasping for breath, while the room cools down.

No doubt there are other ways of treating your rooms, and believe it or not, your library has books on the subject. But this one is generally accepted as being a pretty good method which can be adapted using carpet instead of roofing felt. You could even stick Cosiwrap loft insulation to your walls first, then carry on with the sandwich, but again without the felt.

All the necessary materials are available more or less anywhere, often at discount. However, you won't find sound attenuators in your local DIY store.

# chapter 3
## Pub Drumming Masterclass

To some a joke, to others a living, to all a unifying and levelling experience, pub drumming is the tiny acorn from which many great drumming oaks have grown. The smell of beer, toilets ("just set up here son, next to the gents..."), and the blithe, drunken indifference of the drinkers — who'd want to play Wembley when the boozer is on offer?

But it's a fine art, a delicate balancing act, a whole discipline that is so easy to ignore. Like the trainee tabla player, the budding pub drummer may not touch his instrument for years, least of all in public, as he/she only ever gets the Landlord's answer machine, and the kit is left permanently in the car (steal me, please, I'm insured). Pub drumming may look easy, and whilst we all want to play like Dave Weckl, the punters down at the Dog and Duck really don't want us to. What they want is pub classics with a solid beat. 'Baker Street' by Gerry Rafferty, 'Don't Stop Me Now (I'm Having A Good Time)' by Queen, 'Is This The Way To Amarillo' by Tony Christie, knocked out with a fat, unrelenting beat and full of theatrical fills. This is why it's essential that you take as big a kit as you can, not for playing purposes, but as a shield in case the drinkers turn. This does not apply to pub jazz players, as the idea with pub jazz is, as we all know, to clear the bar area in the minimum time possible ("This one's called Frankie and Johnny..." Clarinets... Arrgh, kill me!).

In the traditional 'high-tech duo' there are, obviously, three of you. Due to entertainment license laws the singer is there purely as a 'guest', as the pub will usually only have a license for two performers. Chas and Dave's drummer is their 'guest' for these reasons — now there's an invitation.

There are three rules with pub drumming:

**1.** *drown out the singer.*

**2.** *drown out the keyboardist.*

**3.** *there are no rules*
(...'Trane, Bird, Roger Whitaker etc. etc.).

These rules are to be adhered to at all times — it is expected of you in fact. Bear in mind that all this time you are trying to drown yourself in lager. Not only that, you must start off every number with a "One, two, three, four..." that bears no relation to the tempo or even time signature that follows. Bang your sticks together, arms as stiff as possible, elbows locked. Anything in three, or its multiples ('House of the Rising Sun' anyone?) must be performed as shambolically as possible, including as lengthy as possible a switch from brushes to sticks. This is a fine art that few drummers get right. Leaving your sticks on the floor tom is all very well, but you might want to hit it, and the strange rattling and buzzing you get when you do that is awful, so the only place to put them is on the floor, next to your pint. Naturally, while you're down there to pick up sticks you have a sip of your lager — all right, all right, a good guzzle — and to make up for this uncharacteristic silence kick off your hi-hats to cover the gap. When the sticks arrive, all that is required is the fill from 'In The Air Tonight'; and don't worry, you'll make it fit.

Being a pub musician is tricky. Queen's post-Freddie release only topped the charts because of the hordes of pub musicians who rushed out to buy this seance on vinyl, realising that Queen is a pub essential. The punters love it, though they do understand if you miss out the middle of 'Bohemian Rhapsody'.

The ability to play slow ballads must become second nature, but as there's only you and the keyboardist, you've got to overplay. This is again tricky, but accords you, the pub drummer, with fantastic power. Couple dancing together, smooching. You've had your eye on him/her all night, and maybe in the break after your second set you were going over to make small talk ("Yeah, well this isn't the whole of my kit..."). They're getting on far too well, you're never going to get him/her back to your room to look at your Fan-toms. So what do you do? Double time — take the band round the chorus at double speed (this does sound quite good) and it'll stuff up any smooching that's going on. Try it, it works.

Moreover, the dress code is very strict: a T-shirt and jeans and nothing but. And make sure that the T-shirt is not one of these new-fangled one-size-fits-all; no, what you need is a small T-shirt that will show you in your full glory, especially when you take your number. You didn't know? Oh yeah, this has replaced the solo you used to have to do whilst the singer went the bar to relax his punished vocal

chords with a pint and adjust his quiff. This means that you have got to be capable of playing and singing at the same time, and seeing as you're the singer, you have to drown yourself out (rule 1). This is harder than it sounds, because if you're anything like me, the louder you play the louder you sing or shout, probably, and you end up in a bizarre volume spiral with yourself. And all this without monitors — no-one said it would be easy.

These are of course simple essentials for survival in the pub-dog-eat-crisp world of pub music. Different drummers' experiences will be different, and in the festive season anything can happen, so with any luck this brief dispatch from the snugs and saloons of the country will help you on your way. You are the entertainment that no-one has paid for, which means that to them you are worth nothing, and that you are little more than musical toilet paper — there but not essential to every visit. But do not let this get you down. On New Year's Eve, as you bang out 'Auld Lang Syne' you'll notice that none of them know the words either, but it's you that has the beat, you are in charge. Not only that, you're staying for the lock-in. Cheers! And please take your glasses back to the bar.

○ **Stage set at the Dog And Duck**

# chapter 4
# Rhythms of the world

## Latin Primer

When detailing any account of a musical form which is as eclectic in style and colour as the one we've come to know as Latin American, it's easy to find yourself in a comparatively rare position these days — one of feeling a genuine warmth and optimism for the human spirit.

### ROOTS AND SCOPE

The study of the rich vein of musical development which suffused the South American sub-continent a century or so ago, and from there, through the United States and the rest of the world, is a classic example of the 'melting pot' syndrome so often encountered when a number of disparate cultures are merged together under conditions of relative hardship.

As is frequently the case, however, trying to establish a coherent order or structure to this mélange becomes something of a nightmare, precisely because of this diversity of influence. The cross-fertilisation of cultures that can emerge from an area containing some 30 separate countries (each using variations of two different languages, and having firmly established

roots with two other continents as diverse as Africa and America), becomes quite overwhelming in its complexity. It has in fact led to a musical genre which clearly could never be unravelled to the extent of providing precise genealogy, or, indeed, anything other than a rather superficial record of its major lines of evolution.

The situation is further complicated by virtue of the fact that much of the evolution of Latin American music took place during this century — a century which has seen the emergence of continuously improving systems of communication.

This has resulted in the development of styles and ideas from cultures which absorbed strong Latin influences, being 'fed back' into the melting pot of Latin America — completing a cycle, the beginning of which it is quite impossible to establish. However, given the sheer wealth of rhythmic concepts inherent in this fascinating musical pastiche (not to mention the extraordinary variety and number of the instruments it embraces), it would take a great many books the size of this one to cover every aspect. So here, I won't be attempting any precise definitions of rhythms and dance structures; rather, I'll be looking at the major developments and

✪ Bashiri Johnson

✪ Lenny Castro

✪ Jodi Linscott

better known examples of the genre.

It is an unfortunate fact that the closest most musicians get to Latin America rhythms is through the type of drum machines that were popular some years back. Most self-respecting drummers were quite vociferous in condemning them, and to this day, serious programmers and composers avoid them like the plague. You know the type of thing — twenty or 30 preset rhythms of the Samba, Rumba, Foxtrot and Tango variety — difficult to know whether to play it or radio the police on it.

Given pop music's penchant for plagiarism, it is quite surprising that the potential gold mine which Latin American music represents, especially in terms of dance rhythms, has remained largely untapped. With the obvious exception of Santana during the Seventies and bands like Kid Creole and the Coconuts, Carmel, Gloria Estafan and Matt Bianco a bit more recently, pop music seems to have largely ignored Latin America as a mainstream influence. The UK has really only absorbed any Latin influence through its assimilation into, firstly, American jazz, and the popular music styles. Even at this level, its effect should not be underrated. It has by no means been as pervasive as R&B, soul and reggae have, for example, given the UK's usual open-armed approach to cultural influence. The same, thankfully, cannot be said of the States, which in the course of the last 60 or 70 years has acted as a huge watershed for Latin music, becoming one of its principle markets and absorbing it into its own more indigenous music forms, to the extent that it is now quite integral to American music, having been further sustained by the mass immigration of Latinos from many countries into the US during this century.

Fortunately, for the purposes of this article, we can quite reasonably limit our examination of Latin American music to four of the 30 or so countries which comprise the South American mainland and Caribbean islands — these being Brazil, Cuba, Mexico and Argentina. This is largely because it was only after Latin music's infiltration into American culture, via the streets of New York, that the further fusion of styles from countries like Puerto Rico, Haiti, and the Dominican Republic occurred and helped its transition into what we now call 'salsa'. However, even after this apparent simplification, we have to take into consideration the influences brought to bear on these countries by the three continents we have mentioned.

## INFLUENCES

In the case of Brazil and Cuba for example, the African influence was particularly strong. However, whereas Cuba drew its major European influence from Spain (as did the greater part of Latin America), Brazil historically was aligned with Portugal. This factor has helped define the Brazilian style as being more laid-back and fluid than is the case with Cuban music, which is characterised by a more driving beat and a 'harder' edge.

In Argentina and Mexico, though black Africa did make its presence felt in the musical development of both countries, it was found to a much lesser degree in Cuba or Brazil, with the result that Spanish and European music was by far the more dominant influence, reflected in a perhaps greater emphasis on melody than on rhythm — more than is the case in much Latin American music. Also to be considered is the influence of Amerindian culture on mainland Latin America, although this isn't particularly evident in Cuba or any of the Caribbean islands.

However, whatever the culture or influences, the spark that lit the flame of Latin American music grew from a wonderfully off-chance meeting of two very different musical forms which merged quite elegantly over a period of decades. The entire foundation of Latin music was born out of the ability of complex African polyrhythms to fuse with Spanish and Portuguese music quite seamlessly. This was principally because of Spain and Portugal's Arabic heritage which allowed their music to blend with African rhythms without trying to impose a four-beats-per-measure structure on it, as happened with most Afro-American fusions.

## CUBA

It's probably fair to say that the heart of black Africa beats more insistently in Cuban music than in any other Latin style. Indeed, the fundamental rhythmic pattern of Cuban music — the clave — is a 3/2 structure which mirrors quite accurately the 'call and response' composition of much African music.

The most enduring influence in Cuban music was a dance style known as the 'habernera', and was derived from folk dances originating in Spain. It forms the basis of much Cuban (and therefore Latin American) music. However, probably more interesting from a rhythmic point of view, was the 'son', a song style actually developed in Cuba which formed the basis of what became known as the Rumba — a dance craze which swept America following the enormous success of Moises Simon's 'The Peanut Vendor' in 1930.

In its original form it was performed on instruments such as the 'tres' (a nine-stringed guitar), trumpet, bongos, maracas and claves, and played by seven-piece bands known as 'septetos'. Its rhythm was very noticeably syncopated with a characteristic 'chuka-chung' style.

Together with the habernera and the son, the other major influence in Cuban music was a more popular, melodic style of song, which proved very successful in the US during the early part of this century, the best examples coming from such composers as Amadeo Roldan and Ernesto Lecuona.

Cuban music, generally, was probably the most influential of all the Latin styles which filtered into the US, and to this day is probably the most enduring.

The US strain of Latin, salsa, which took root on the streets of New York, is principally a direct descendant of Cuban styles, and, is played by bands closely resembling Cuban outfits which developed alongside the emergent music during the first decades of this century. Again, these bands were many and varied in terms of composition, but gradually, three distinct styles developed. The first of these were the septetos and sextetos who performed the sons style of song mentioned earlier. Secondly, there were the 'charangas', who were in effect small dance orchestras featuring violins, flute, piano, bass and timbales. They played the more formal, structured, popular songs of the day, and, it could be said, appealed more to the upper stratas of Cuban society.

In contrast, the third major form of ensemble (which emerged during the 1930s) was an altogether earthier type of outfit known as 'conjutos'. They developed from black parade bands, and adopted a much more percussive, African style, featuring — besides vocals — trumpets, piano, bass, conga drums and bongos.

They existed at much more of a street level than did charangas, and did much more to introduce the more African-based rhythms such as the Congolese 'mamba' to the public's attention, particularly in the US, and notably through one man — a blind Afro-Cuban named Arsenio Rodriguez.

Eventually, the charanga bands were to adopt much of the style of the conjuntos, and it can be argued that they had probably the most lasting effect in terms of popularising Cuban, Latin American music.

## BRAZIL

The softer, more fluid styles of rhythm encountered in Brazilian music, can to a large extent be attributed to the strong Portuguese traditions which became Brazil's inheritance. Indeed, it can be quite fascinating to listen to Cuban and Brazilian versions of the same rhythmic pattern. While the Cuban percussionist would adopt a hard, straightforward 'on-the-beat' style, the Brazilian performance would be characterised by a subtler approach, with a change in accentuation giving a lighter, more relaxed feel.

Though Brazilian music has perhaps not been as consistently influential as that of Cuba, it has, through the US, been responsible for several major rhythm or 'dance' styles. The most noticeable among them is the 'Maxixe' — a habernera-influenced version of an earlier Afro-Brazilian dance, the much better known 'Samba' which has dominated Brazilian music since the 1940s, and the comparatively recent Bossa Nova — a 'purpose made' dance rhythm created during the 1950s. Of the three, it's really only the Samba and the Bossa Nova which have had any lasting influence, although the Maxixe is believed to be the forerunner of the Samba, and therefore should at least be mentioned.

The Samba provides the rhythm for most Brazilian carnival dancing, and was to a large extent developed from the percussion-orientated 'schools' of the Rio de Janeiro carnival. It has a jazzy, 2/4, shuffling rhythm, and is encountered in a number of different versions, the most popular of which is the 'carioca' style, again developed in Rio, and which has become the basis of much international Latin pop music.

The Bossa Nova, which to some extent was a sequel to the Samba, was in fact a creation of a number of jazz-orientated musicians and poets during the 1950s. It was an altogether simpler style of Afro-Brazilian dance rhythms which made it easier for musicians outside Latin America to assimilate and play. Indeed, it could be considered as 'white' Latin, being cooler and more sophisticated than most Afro-Latin styles.

## ARGENTINA

In the early part of this century, a Latin dance style emerged from the streets of Buenos Aires which was to become probably the first international dance craze. The 'Tango' initially gained popularity in Argentina during the 1910s, despite the fact that it was considered rather steamy — even by Latin dance standards. Within a couple years it had begun to infect the US via Broadway, though, again, it was in the face of considerable outcry from 'polite' American society. However, its popularity continued unabated, and it was soon to be found in Paris and most other European cities. It is another habernera-derived rhythm, with its basis in African music while drawing quite heavily on European harmonic influences.

In this case, it was the quite large Italian community that had established in Argentina, which helped to define its European qualities, in addition to the more usual Spanish influences. It has been argued that the quite dramatic nature of the Tango is reminiscent of the drama in the operatic style of much Italian music, and it is probably fair to say that it was the over-emphasis of this trait in the Tango that led to it becoming almost comic in its interpretation in latter years, which was regrettable since it started life as quite a strident African roots rhythm.

## MEXICO

The cross-fertilisation of musical genres alluded to at the start of this article, is nowhere more evident that in Mexican music. Sadly, from a rhythmic point of view this has meant that Mexican music lacks much of the colour and urgency that characterises the rhythmic structure of most Latin music, and this has probably been due to the heavy influence of European rhythms which pervade early Mexican music — the waltz and the polka being particularly evident.

It was also unfortunate that when African dance rhythms did begin to make inroads into Mexican music during the early part of this century, they were almost totally derived from Cuba, and as a result tended to be already 'defined'. Melodically however, Mexico was probably the most highly developed of all the Latin countries, and this combined with it's geographical location (directly between the US and the rest of the Latin mainland), conspired to make it very much the 'river delta' in terms of the flow of Latin American music into the United States.

# Eastern Beat

To those in the know, the name Kerala (with the accent on the first syllable) might suggest one of two things. First, perhaps the image of a lush, green, semi-tropical landscape full of rivers and inland waterways, peopled by highly literate and very outgoing residents. If not that, then maybe the first place in the world to freely elect a communist state government, which it did in 1957. Its cultural life has, until recently, been less apparent. Dance/drama forms such as kathakali, kutiyattam, mohiniattam have been seen in the west, but the purely musical styles remain more elusive.

Thyambaka is a ritual drum music found in the state of Kerala, located in the south west of India. It exclusively features the chenda, a barrel-shaped drum worn across one shoulder and played with curved sticks. The chenda is about 20″ tall and 13″ across. It is made from the very hard wood of the jack fruit tree and has two heads, both made from a cow's stomach. The bottom head is only occasionally employed. The vast majority of the action is in the super-tight top side. The heads come ready fashioned from their traditional makers, the local leather workers, in one piece including a wooden rim. The fitting of a new head is a time honoured and physically exacting process needing two experienced people. There are yards and yards of (nowadays) nylon coated rope that need constant threading, pulling and slacking until the optimum sound is obtained. There are one or two makers who are now experimenting with metal tension rods, but change comes slowly.

Normally, a full thyambaka ensemble will feature between eight and ten players, with the focus on one main drummer who will have many opportunities to show his dexterity and invention during the 90 minutes or so of a programme.

The geometrically developing structure starts slowly and sparsely and builds to an awesome intensity through four main sections. it requires great physical strength and stamina from the participants — a chenda weighs around 8kg.

The talam, or structural shape, is kept by eddatalum (heavy bronze cymbals), while various other chendas, differently tuned, will have important time-keeping roles. Within this framework, the principal player(s) will play precise structures as well as improvised passages. In a double or triple thyambaka the other featured players will respond in kind to the rhythmic callings of the most senior player. Occasionally, quadruple or quintuple thyambakas have been known, but these are very rare. The supporting players may be the choice of the featured artist or of the organising committee of the particular venue. Either way, the musicians all know the required repertoire and don't need to rehearse, although the more unified groups will be the ones with intimate knowledge of each other's playing. The music is usually performed at Hindu temples during the festival season, from November to May, but

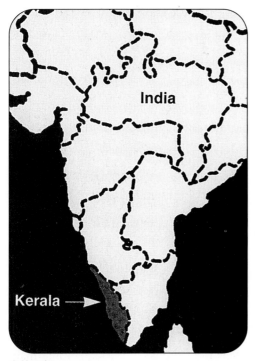

○ Kerala

hand stick technique is of a more familiar up-down motion, but in thyambaka this stick is dispensed with in favour of the bare hand, adorned only by hardened rice rings around the fingers to provide that extra crack to the sound. The left hand of an experienced practitioner is a disaster area, with welts and weals bearing hard evidence of a life of heavy beating.

Thyambaka is far less familiar in the UK. Ten years ago a group performed in London's Holland Park at the Indian Ocean Music Festival, but since then nothing. The chenda is more often seen on these shores as accompaniment to the kathakali (or for theyyam or kuttchypuddy), although the two roles require very different approaches. Also, players may perform in chenda melam — another, slightly simplified, ritual drum form which can contain anything from ten to 100 players.

I have just returned from a spell in Kerala where I spent some time receiving guidance in thyambaka from perhaps its greatest contemporary exponent, Mattanur Sankaran Marar. Amidst his hectic current schedule, he found time for my daily lesson where, although I have studied chenda before, I was returned to the fat sticks and stone division in order to properly cover the necessary groundwork.

In a field of extraordinarily high standards, Sankaram is generally considered to be the man in the ascendancy right now. Although only forty or so, his relaxed, very clear playing is widely acclaimed not only in Kerala but throughout India. He has numerous commendations and awards that bear testament to this. He is also grooming the next generation of players. His sons, sixteen and thirteen, already perform widely in Kerala, displaying enviable facility and deftness rarely witnessed in boys of that age. Their skills would always provide me with a chastening reminder of my own more measured progress.

I watched many thyambaka

has no overtly religious significance.

The training can start from age six to eight, and consists of daily two or three hour sessions. Rhythms are first learnt vocally, then translated onto a stone surface played with heavy, oversized sticks (for muscle development), and later onto the chenda itself. Each main stock rhythm can be practised at four speeds, starting slowly and doubling three times, then coming back down again, increasing first speed, doubling, and so on, until one finds one's limit. In the hands of an expert, the fourth speed can be hard to hear, let alone play.

A chenda player can achieve extraordinary speed, an ability acquired through rigorous training. In the West, the percussionist will normally play up-down strokes with the right hand; the chenda player draws the curved right hand stick towards and away from the body, across the drum head — the wrist motion is fundamentally different this way. The left programmes, most of which occurred in the cool of evening or the dead of night. Once, I hired an auto-rickshaw to ferry me the round trip of 40 miles to a thyambaka at Ongallur, between Palakkad (Palghat) and Kozhikode (Calicut), deep in the cultural heartland, to see three consecutive single thyambakas. The temple site was next to a funfair, whose activities were winding down to give way to the night's music. The audience was large, mixed, and very knowledgeable, and there were no stray mics, no cheap PA, and no concrete walls or baffles to distort the mighty sound.

Guruvayoor Hari presented his thyambaka first. His was a performance of obvious physical effort and hard graft. He was very well received. As his group left the stage on one side, Sankaran's party entered it from the back — no breaks in the business tonight. Now however, the mood is lighter; very relaxed with lots of eye contact and smiles among the musicians. Sankaran was warmly applauded and then proceeded to demolish all memory of the previous performers in a set of staggering intensity and invention. Lastly, Sankaran's own guru, Vasudevan, another master of the relaxed school of playing, performed sublimely. The rupee notes were changing hands at a furious rate, from punter to punter, in a time honoured and ostentatious show of appreciation. While it is not about competition, there's an edge to the proceedings, much of it generated by partisan groups in the audience. Other seasoned watchers meticulously clapped rhythm, scrutinising the accuracy of the three performers. Everyone, including small children (and the auto-rickshaw driver) stayed the course of four and a half hours of solid drumming — and dug it, too!

Sankaran Marar has the perfect day job. He teaches chenda at his local government high school. It is deemed sufficiently important to have a resident teacher. His predecessor in the job, V. Damodaran Nair,

now retired, gave me my first chenda lesson fourteen years ago. Students do not necessarily continue this specialist study unless a particular aptitude is shown. The world of chenda playing has traditionally been a totally male preserve, but with high school students numbering girls as well, it could be that the next generation of players will see women taking part in thyambaka too.

I met some Geordie backpackers in Trivandrum who described beach life in Goa as 'kicking'. I doubt they had the slightest idea of where the real pulse of South India was coming from.

## On the dhol

One of the amazing things about Indian music is the fact that it has been changed very little over the centuries by passing trends and fashions. This is so not only for the musical system, but also for the instruments' design and manufacture. Age old techniques demanding great skill and patience are still being used in an age where machines are dominant. Even so, the intricate craftsmanship is beginning to die out. The instrument maker is often struggling to earn a good living, and as time ensues families with long lineages of craftsmen behind them are turning away from the craft as younger generations go into more commercial lines. Sad as it is, it's inevitable just so long as the criterion is maximum profit for minimum pay out. What motivation would someone have to work for months making an instrument that it took them years to learn how to make when they can do business studies and treble their money?

In India and the UK there is one man who is very aware of this problem and has devoted his life to upkeeping the standards of the old traditional ways of making Indian instruments, and to seeing to it that the craftsmen are paid well enough to want to continue. Harjit Singh Shah is based in London but has a large factory and manufacturing plant for Indian instruments in Delhi and Utra Pardesh in India. For twenty-four generations his family have been involved in the music business in India. Having studied the finer details of instrument making with some of the top exponents of the craft in India, Harjit set up his business, JAS Musicals.

Traditionally very few machines are used in making Indian instruments, most of the processes being carried out by hand. One exception to this is the lathe used in the turning of the drum shells. From the chopping and sawing of the tree right down to the carving and skin making, the rest of the job is done entirely by hand.

I'm going to look at the manufacture of a dhol drum, from when it was a tree until its arrival on the shop shelf.

The dhol is a double-ended, barrel shaped drum held around the neck and played with two cane sticks. Traditionally, both heads are made from goat skin laced together over the shell by one piece of rope threaded through the edges of both skins. As with many Indian double-ended drums, one head is tuned to generate the bass tones while the other head geared towards the treble. For this purpose, one skin is be made slightly thicker than the other.

Sizes range from 12" to 27" deep, sometimes even 30", but you would have to have seriously long arms to play a drum of that size. The treble end ranges from between 12" to 14" in diameter, but the most favoured head size is 13". The bass head is usually slightly bigger than the treble head. Unlike most Indian drums though, the bass end has no resonating patch to assist the bass tone of the drum — drums such as the dholak and the nall have a massalla (paste) inside the bass skin which brings the pitch down considerably. There is also no

patch used on the treble skin, unlike with drums such as tabla, nall, mridangam, and phakawaj.

Nowadays some dhol players substitute the goat skin on the treble end of the drum for a plastic head. This is tuned by means of a series of tension bolts. The bass end is usually kept as goat skin and is still laced through its hoop, the difference being that it laces around the nut-boxes at the treble end. This adds a sensible degree of practicality to the drum whilst keeping its traditional appearance, and is an idea originally thought up by Harjit Singh Shah himself.

The shell of a dhol is made from one piece of wood, ideally a hardwood such as shesham, which is similar to teak. The harder the wood, the sharper and clearer the sound.

In India, all the tree chopping is done by the government who hold massive tree auctions attended by hundreds, sometimes thousands of people. Over the last four years the prices have risen by at least three times. The trees are bought unseasoned; it must look like Sloane Square after The Chelsea Flower Show.

Harjit is one instrument maker who always attends the auctions in person to choose the right wood. He then gets it delivered to his seasoning plant outside a small village in Utra Pardesh where the tree is left whole in the open air for one year. This part of the country, besides being beautifully scenic, also has very uncompromising seasons and therefore gives the wood a thorough seasoning. It can get as cold as 2-3°C, and as hot as 49°C. This, coupled with the rainy season, gives the wood exposure to many changes in climate.

After seasoning, the tree is taken to the second factory in Naraina in Delhi, Central India. It's then sawn into smaller cross sections by hand by two individuals and a saw that would make Rolf Harris wince. This is a very long winded and backbreaking job, but not half as backbreaking as the next stage: carving the block of wood into a general drum shape with a big axe called a kulhari. This part of the process can take up to two days.

Next comes the only part of the process involving machines. The drum-shaped solid block is placed on a lathe; at this point, the shell has a smaller block cut from its centre with a sharp metal instrument. This smaller version then gets put onto another lathe and has an even smaller block cut from its centre. The result is three identical blocks which become dhol, dholak and small tabla respectively, each being smaller than the next one, like a set of Russian dolls. The lathe is then modified to be able to hold the shells for the next part of the process. The outsides are given their final shaping on the lathe and all the decorative carvings are added. These shells are then seasoned for another six months, although this time under a shelter, protected from the sun and rain.

Following this important second seasoning the shells are hand-picked. Not all shells will have survived the process without developing small cracks or splits. These shells are disposed of, only the best getting accepted for the final part of the operation. The shells each receive a final seasoning mixture applied to the inside. This massalla of soil proteins is applied and allowed some time to soak in fully. This final seasoning adds warmth and depth to the final tone of the drum.

Following this the shells receive their coat of varnish and polish, depending on what finish is required. There is a big demand these days for unpolished drums — if the drum has been well seasoned this can be particularly attractive.

Each shell then has its goat skin heads made. Each head is made specifically for each drum because in the second seasoning, depending on the heat, the shells can shrink slightly. The heads have bamboo hoops around which the skin is dried. Holes are made at regular intervals around the edge near the bamboo rim, and the skins are laced together over the shell and tensioned. If the drums are to be exported then I'm assured by the people at JAS that all fine tuning changes are done at their destination. The climatic changes would be too great for such finely tuned instruments to survive. This is important with drums but is a vital necessity with instruments such as the sitar.

After all this time consuming manufacture, the drums are packed into containers in Delhi and then transported by rail to the Indian coast where they begin their sea voyage to Europe. Packing the drums well for a journey like this is almost as important as the attention paid to the manufacturing process. Damaged equipment would be of little use to anybody. Harjit makes special journeys to India to supervise the packing process. Only about five percent of the goods get damaged in transit — usually the more fragile items such as sitars and sarods.

The dhol is played with two sticks, one on each end. The treble end is played with a

○ JAS dhol

○ **Playing the dhol**

thin piece of flexible cane approximately 15″ to 16″ long. The bass end is also played with a piece of cane, but much thicker and bent at 45 degrees for the last two inches of its 15″ to 16″ length. The making and bending of the stick is simply a matter of showing flame to the point at which you want the bend, and the sheer strength of one's hands. I was assured that there is a special device to make this easier, but it's still very impressive to watch.

The history of the drum dates back many centuries to when it was used by town criers. The reason becomes quite evident when you hear it, for it can be astonishingly loud. As time went on it became integrated into harvest festivals, and in fields where the locals sang, danced and took care of their crops. The rhythms were then mutated into a dance format, giving rise to the traditional roots of folk dance in the Punjab. This is actually the true roots of bhangra. If you look at the dance patterns of bhangra you will see lots of choreography which draws reference back to these early folk dances which were literally born from synchronised cropping movements in the field.

The dhol began to be known in the UK in the early Seventies and started to get the attention it deserved when Alaap, the pioneers of Asian pop, began to use a dhol in their group for the first time. Johnny Kalsi was the man who got the gig and has kept it ever since. Dhol players were few and far between at the time, but since then Johnny has opened up The Dhol Foundation and now has well over a hundred students. His dream is to make the drum more accessible and known to a wider audience, and to open up teaching establishments all over the UK. The foundation also have their first CD planned for later in 1996. Besides this he maintains a healthy session career, including recent projects with the Asian Dub Foundation.

Another one of Johnny's priorities is to teach women the dhol. This is quite against social convention and clearly deserving of a lot of encouragement.

Dhol playing technique involves playing the bass end with the large stick and the treble end with the thin stick. It's interesting when you begin to compare the style in which Indian drums are played. Whether from the north or the south of the country all the drums have distinct similarities within their playing techniques. For example, the bass end of the dhol has the open 'Ge' sound and the closed 'Ke' sound as would be found on dholak or tabla, the only difference being that you use a stick instead of a hand or finger. This is the reason for the bend in the dhol stick. By playing it with the top section flat on the head you get the closed 'Ke' sound. The 'Ge' sound is played with a severe whiplash motion involving the whole arm pulling the stick away from the head and then quickly back onto it.

The treble side meanwhile can be compared to the tabla or the mridangam. It has the 'Na' rim sound ('Nam' on the mridangam), the 'Tin' inner ring sound ('Dim' on the mridangam), and the closed 'Te' sound ('Ti' on the mridangam).

Admittedly there is not so much differentiation between the sounds as on the tabla or mridangam, nor is there as much subtlety, but the general starting point of the technique is basically the same. It doesn't end with the single sounds. A lot of the patterns are based on similar technicalities and use similar concepts. The general rule of thumb with these drums is that the more you find a drum in classical Indian music, the more intellectually developed will the techniques and patterns be. This makes neither way better or worse, and anyone who is snobby and pedantic about such things is being foolish. What we can say is that they come from the same root.

The basic building blocks of the drum hinge on these five sounds: 'Na', 'Tin' and 'Te' on the treble side, and 'Ge' and 'Ke' for the bass.

We then get compound words by playing two sounds simultaneously. These would be thus:

'Na' + 'Ge' = 'Dha'
'Tin' + 'Ge' = 'Dhin'
'Te' + 'Ge' = 'Dhe'

Traditionally there would be no compound word for the combination of the 'Ke' and 'Na' sounds, but Johnny Kalsi calls this 'Kin' for his students. Once you know where all these sounds come on the drum skins you begin to learn short phrases of words that you can then play on the drum. It's truly a great system and well worth learning, even if you don't want to become a traditional Indian drummer. If your appetite has been whetted then you could always contact The Dhol Foundation: Johnny Kalsi, 0181 574 8316, or 0197 363 6367.

## Pothole Surfers

Not at all a membranophone, but rather part idiophone, part percussion aerophone, the udu drum has been around for centuries, tempting subtle rhythms from the master drummers of Nigeria and modern day percussionists alike. Udu quite simply means 'pot' in the language of the Ibo tribe of Nigeria, and a pot it literally is. Pots and percussion seem to go together rather well. Pop down to the garden centre and see for yourself; tap a few and you will soon hear how some of them resonate. You'll probably get a few odd looks, maybe even get thrown out, but what the hell, if it's all part of the educational experience of life, then it must be of benefit.

Turn on to classical Carnatic music from South India and you'll hear a pot called the ghatam. Listen to pot players such as T. H. Vinayakram with Shakti, and you'll be blown away. In a more current vein, artists as varied as Miles Davis, Sting and Jan Garbarek have all used udus on some of their world tours. If pots have been used so effectively as drums for so long and across so many continents, then there must be something in them, other than air.

Although both Indian and Nigerian pots are made of clay, the udu differs from the ghatam in one very important feature, the number of holes. The ghatam has only one opening on its top, like a normal water pot. The drum stands about 14" high, has no neck, and is round in shape apart from the flat playing surface which leads up to the hole on top. This opening is about 5" in diameter. Traditional players spend most of the time playing the outside of the pot with their fingers, wrists and thumbs, and use the airy 'whoof whoof' sound, created by displacing air in the pot by hitting over the hole, very sparingly.

The udu, on the other hand, is more of a side-hole pot drum, and has two holes about 3" in diameter — one on the top and one on the side. Having said this, I have seen pictures of ancient Nigerian pot drums which have looked radically different, some having very wide holes on top and tiny holes in the body of the drum. Traditionally, it is more spherical in shape than the ghatam, and has a narrow neck which leads up to the hole on its top. The udu also comes in different sizes, and traditionally would make up a family of four drums in the same way as many other sets of African drums. These four pots range in size from 18cm to 40cm in height. Each drum would have a different pitch, the largest being the bass voice and the smallest the treble voice. Some believe the deep, haunting sound lured from the sound chamber by the bare hand to be the voices of the ancestors, causing it to have significant involvement in religious ceremonies.

The origins of the drum have been traced back to central and southern Nigeria, and it has been found that, although we're using the term udu, the side-hole pot drum is known by many different names, depending on the tribal areas and particular ceremonies in which it is used.

The traditional method for making an udu is to pound a lump of soft earthen clay over a firm spherical form known as a lump mould. The lump of clay is placed on the mould and tempted into shape around it with a large flat stone. It is then carefully beaten to uniform thickness with handmade paddles a little like huge wooden spoons or ping pong bats. Following this it is cut down to a half-sphere on the mould. This half-sphere becomes the bottom half of the drum. The top half is then constructed using the coil method, which involves building up long lengths of clay one upon another before squeezing, paddling and shaping them up and into the sides of the drum. The important thing during this process is to make sure that the sides are of uniform thickness — this is of vital importance to the quality of sound of the finished instrument.

Building up the sides in this manner can be as slow as one and a half inches per day,

and can take as long as fourteen days to complete. Following this, the side hole is cut and the drum is hand-rubbed with a smooth stone to seal the surface. This has the effect of giving the drum a deep lustre without using any type of glaze which might make it less resonant. The drum is then dried under strictly controlled conditions before it undergoes two firings — the first at a specific temperature for hardness and sound quality, and the second in an outdoor kiln. It is removed from this kiln whilst glowing hot, and plunged into a container of combustible material. Once removed from the ashes, it reveals its traditional black lustre finish. The whole process is said to take at least one month.

The work done during the early paddling construction work has one very interesting consequence to note; that is, the reformation of the tiny platelets which make up the clay. The continuous pounding compresses aligns and interlocks the platelets into a strong, dense body with similar properties to a hand-hammered cymbal. The end result is a strong, resonant pot with two holes, and it is the shape of said pot which will be our next area of focus. We could call it a single hollow sphere with a straight neck of calculated length and width relative to the volume of the chamber. Helmholtz resonator is the general term used for resonators such as this with non-tubular air chambers communicating with the outside air through a single aperture (presupposing there is only one hole). If you see what I mean...

Since the early 1980s the existence of the udu drum has been developed, transformed and made altogether more accessible thanks to the efforts of one man, Frank Giorgini. With a Bachelor of Industrial Design, a Bachelor in fine Arts in Education, and a Master of Fine Arts in Ceramics, along with his full time ceramic sculpture studio and gallery in Freehold, NY, Giorgini supplies the whole percussion world with udu drums.

✪ The udu: a strong, resonant pot with two holes

Where is the divide between art and the instrument? Why shouldn't one make an instrument into a work of art at the same time? Giorgini must be the only drum maker in the world to get two of his instruments taken on by one of the major art galleries in the world as permanent exhibits. Pop into the Metropolitan Museum of Art on Fifth Avenue, NY and see for yourselves. If you can't get there then you can always try the Nassau County Museum of Fine Arts in Roslyn or the Art Awareness Gallery in Lexicon, NY. It certainly brings another dimension to drum making.

Since his involvement in 1985 with master Nigerian potter Abbas Ahuwan, Giorgini has spent his time developing the udu drum. That has manifested in a number of ways. Besides making them stronger and more durable (apparently not one has broken under a player's hand), he has introduced a whole new range of udu designs. Some seem to look like bowling balls, while others look like molten dumb bells. Others look quite simply like nothing you've ever seen before.

The drums can be played in a number of ways. For example, by sitting cross legged on the floor, one can put the drum in one's lap with one hand over each hole. The hand on the top controls the pitch, while the other plays over the hole on the side. One can use the palms, finger tips, slap in the fashion of conga playing, or even play them with mallets or brushes. It is also possible to stand-mount udu drums and play them standing up. Some of the contraptions for this purpose are quite extraordinary in their own right, and could probably find their way into an art gallery on the merit of their obscurity. Anyway, most percussionists could immediately get a result on an udu drum, but particularly players who are used to intricate passages with their fingers, i.e. tabla players or Middle Eastern percussionists. Udu drums have even been compared to tabla in as much as some of the glissandos that can be produced are very similar to the speaking voice of the bass tabla.

Having spent years developing his drumming pots, Frank Giorgini decided he wanted to increase his knowledge and went for some further field studies in Nigeria. "It was a bit like a scene from a National Geographic article," said Mrs Giorgini about their journey from the States to Nigeria with a 15lb udu pot in tow, to arrive and be granted an audience with an important person in a mud hut. "It really was a great honour for everyone." Evidently the transfer of information went both ways. the master Nigerian potter was so fascinated by the shine on Frank's drum that he got him to repeat his method several times over until he had memorised it. During and since that trip, Frank worked and continues to work on many new designs.

The pressures of time and increasing demand for Giorgini's pots finally led him to develop a second range of drums, the first range being his handmade specialist drums. So complex is the workload for these that he can only make 30 a year. This range is called the Traditional Handmade series and includes a set going up in size from small to large as in the family set mentioned earlier. The second set is the Udu Claytone series. This is a series of moulded drums combining a special clay formula with modern production methods. The same drums are available in both the Claytone and Traditional series.

Further developments are leading to even more elaborate looking drums. For example, it might be interesting to look at the transformation the kim kim clay drum underwent at the hands of Giorgini. These clay drums, along with a number of other side-hole drums, shekere, a woodblock and a large clay drum played with a leather paddle, provided the orchestral accompaniment to the Women's Wing choir of the Evangelical Churches of West Africa. This drum was basically a double-chambered pot which looked rather like a dumb bell. The drum had a hole in each chamber and was played vertically, with one hand hitting the top hole while the other held the middle and changed the pitch by moving the bottom hole on and off the thigh. Giorgini experimented, making it larger and larger until it became too large to be played in the traditional manner and had to be played horizontally with a hand on each end, like a double-ended Indian drum. He also changed the shape of the chambers to make the bass and treble more distinct from one another, and curved the tubular middle section so the drum had both its playing surfaces upright. The result, as you can imagine, is far from the norm.

With further new designs planned, the world looks like it's going to become a much more udu place. They are not easy to get hold of in the UK, but you could always contact Frank direct in New York: Udu Drum, rt. 67, Box 126, Freehold, NY 12431 USA. Tel: (518) 634 2488.

## The Swiss Account

This is the situation: it's 4.00am on a bitingly cold February morning and I'm marching down the street of a Swiss town wearing a large papier maché dog's head and an 18th Century military costume. My logic cells suggest that this is a dream. My ears however tell me otherwise, because I'm also beating the living daylights out of the largest snare drum you've ever seen. There appear to be a considerable number of strangely dressed people doing much the same thing in the vicinity. About 30,000 of them, to be precise.

It could be the set of some vast and ill-advised Soundgarden video; it is in fact the Fasnacht in Basel, Switzerland, the largest and one of the oldest street festivals in Europe, and probably the biggest single drumming event of any kind in the world.

The exact origins of the festival are lost in the murk of the Middle Ages, although some combination of end-of-Winter pagan hooley and civic parade of arms seems closest to the mark. These days Fasnacht is a celebrated and colourful carnival involving elaborate costumes and 24-hour a day partying. The Venice Carnevale meets the Munich Beerfest with a liberal dash of Medieval Mummers Play and Edinburgh Tattoo, if you will.

According to tradition, the shenanigans kick off at the aforementioned 4am on the first Monday of Lent, and run non-stop for 72 hours. Participants in the Fasnacht have to wear full masks and costumes. To show your face while playing is considered the ultimate in bad form. The dog's head I wear is part of the costume of a very special drum group called the Green Dogs, just one of hundreds of bizarrely dressed carnival groups who parade in the streets from bar to bar day and night. The spectacle draws crowds of up to three million to this town on the banks of the Rhine, nudging the French and German borders.

In the UK the Fasnacht remains relatively unknown despite its size. The good burghers of Basel don't exactly court publicity for it, clearly believing that the current level of tourism is about as much as the town can take. And its status among British drummers isn't exactly helped by the fact that the music traditionally played in this carnival is fifes and drums, military style.

Military drumming. The dreaded M word. To most of us military drumming is as foreign as an Estonian restaurant menu. Sure, we all know that the likes of Steve Gadd cut their teeth in the USA corps drumming. But you don't catch Greg Bissonette in a kilt and bearskin, do you? Not outside the privacy of his bedroom, at least.

In Basel, this would be fighting talk. Here, military drumming is a religion followed by thousands. If you've ever wondered what the Swiss do when they're not making cuckoo clocks, eating chocolate or running banks, this is it.

With the annual carnival as encouragement, the Basel kids start learning their rudiments as young as three or four. They join drumming and piping schools, usually run by the bigger carnival performance groups, or Cliques. Nobody knows exactly how many people in Basel play the drum, but 10,000 is a popular figure. Enough for this one town to support half a dozen drum makers.

Basel, more than any other place in the world is Drum City. Five-year olds do it. Grandfathers do it. Spotty adolescents swap paratriplets in the school break. I've known some pretty ugly arguments break out over the exact phrasing of a ratamacue.

The best young drummers from Basel do their military service (compulsory in Switzerland) in the Drum Corps. They come out as fiercely accomplished players. The annual Basel Prize Drumming championship draws big crowds who are knowledgeable to the last flam. To win the competition confers instant star status. If you're a drummer in Basel, you're in good company.

So what's it actually like, this Swiss drumming? Let's start with the best bit.

## THE DRUM

A Basel drum is a piece of sonic weaponry masquerading as a musical instrument. It's about the size of a 17" floor tom, with a diameter anything from 40 to 43 cm. The shell can be made from metal or wood, the hoops from a hard-wearing but light synthetic. It's rope tensioned with a plastic or calf batter, a plastic snare head, and a twin snare with both gut and metal strands which can be adjusted separately. It's hung from a bandolier worn across the body from right shoulder to left hip, and is fastened to the bandolier by a simple knotted thong. It hangs, sloping, in front of you and a little to the left.

Seems a bit low-tech? Don't let looks fool you. Just try clouting it with one of these small tree trunks that Basel drummers call sticks. Woah! Old ladies outside in the street have dropped their shopping; large flocks of birds have taken off from nearby trees. Imagine the dry crispness of a Ludwig Black Beauty combined with the depth and projection of, well, a snare drum that's 17" deep. It's a big, fat sound designed to

reverberate around cobblestone streets and compete with the odd cannon on the battlefields of 18th Century Europe.

The remarkably effective rope tensioning is easy to use and keeps the batter head tight and responsive, while the sensitivity of the twin snares can go down to a whisper. A good Basel drum is a beautifully engineered piece of kit, in the best Swiss tradition. Cheap, however, it's not. A top quality metal-shelled one will set you back at least £500; a birch or maple-shelled wooden one, complete with traditional heraldic paintwork, probably twice that.

## THE MUSIC

Like all military drumming, Basel playing is heavy on technique and rudiments and low on improvisation. At first hearing it's not unlike US fife and drum corps music. There are drum accompaniments to fife tunes, as well as a fine repertoire of drum solos, most designed to be played on the hoof and ranging from the straightforward to the preposterously difficult.

Some of this music dates back a hundred years or more, so you can't exactly make it up as you go along. Basel players learn it by heart. In the early days they learned it phonetically — there is a sophisticated oral language to 'sing' a drum part, differentiating every ruff, flam and roll. Later, various strange, hieroglyphic systems were devised to write the stuff down.

Finally in the 1940s, Dr Fritz Berger, Basel's greatest ever drum teacher, set about recording the Basel repertoire for posterity on conventional staved drum music. His three part work, *Das Basler Trommeln*, is still the definitive collection, a unique record of a unique drumming heritage. It's readily available in Basel, though you'll need a good working knowledge of German to plough through the technique section.

That's the history. But one of the most appealing things about Basel drumming is that it's a living heritage. New marches are being composed all the time. Some stick in the repertoire, some don't.

## THE TECHNIQUE

Unless you happen to have been learning it from the age of three, Basel drumming is not an easy discipline. First there are the problems common to all military drumming. You don't play it just with your wrists, it takes forearms, elbows and shoulders too. There's a minimal use of bounce. The objective is maximum control from pianissimo to fortissimo, a roll that's as smooth as the down on a baby's cheek, flams that sound, as one Basel drummer put it to me, "like when you kick a door shut", and a rock steady rhythmic base. Basel drumming is played completely open, There are no presses or buzzes, nowhere to hide. A nine stroke roll is exactly that. Or else.

But Basel drumming has its own peculiarities, too. Like the fact that rolls at the beginning of phrases are played flammed. So a five stroke roll (RRLLR) actually kicks off with a left hand grace note (l' RRLLR). And it's supposed to sound flammed, too, not like a six stroke roll.

The Swiss have their own rudimentary structure to match the 27 American rudiments. Some, like the Swiss army triplet and the pataflafla will already be similar to British rudiment heads out there. Mastering them all is essential to even the most basic Basel playing, because they're the building blocks of every piece.

## THE FEEL

Remember, too, that you're playing this stuff while walking — often pretty fast — through streets, up hills, down stairs, over bridges, into crowds, carrying a drum the size of a small dustbin. Other groups are playing something completely different very loudly to your right and left. You're in full costume. It's often night-time. And you're wearing a big, heavy mask which

usually has just two small eyeholes to let you see the world. You'll play a repertoire of up to 30 pieces, completely from memory. Now you know why Baslers start playing so young.

There is one last thing, however, that to my ears really sets Basel drumming apart. It actually has a feel, a distinct and unique rhythm. It's best described as a cross between a straight and a dotted crotchet. Like all feels, you won't find it in written music, but it's bred into the bone of every good Basel player, giving their drumming a hypnotic, swinging quality.

That's the attraction of Basel playing for me: it's obsessive, it's loud, and it's got just a pinch of rock 'n' roll in it. And quite frankly, any town that lets me play the drum out in the street at any time of the day or night for three whole days without anyone complaining deserves some big respect. Dog's head, anyone?

# Big in Japan

It was the influence of Chinese and Korean culture between the 5th and 8th Centuries that started the ball rolling. There are records from the 5th century of musicians from Korea attending an Emperor's funeral ceremony. In the 8th century Buddhist services began to be held in the Japanese temples. It was during those few centuries that most of the origins of Japanese percussion arrived in Japan. From then on the Japanese made it their own, incorporating it in their traditional music and theatre, such as gagaku, nogaku, bunraku, and kabuki. Festival music (matsuri bayashi) also contributed to the refinement of techniques and musical forms.

However, professional drumming has only really flourished in Japan since a group of drummers formed a group on Sado

Island in the 1960's. Originally they were called Ondeko-Za which means Devil Drum — 'devil' being used ironically in the same manner as we use 'evil'. After some time there was a divide in musical approaches, and so the group split into two: Ondeko-Za and Kodo.

Before this there were very few professional drumming groups in Japan, but they soon became popular, and now there are over four-hundred professional groups each consisting of between four and twelve performers, sometimes more.

## THE FOUR MAIN TYPES OF DRUM

### MIYA-DAIKO (TEMPLE DRUM)

Carved from a single piece of Japanese elm, the Miya Daiko can range from a 16" by 18" shell to a staggering 6' by seven 7': the smaller weighs a hefty 20 kilos, while the larger cannot be lifted by two grown men. The cost of these drums is also gigantic — they can cost anything from £3,000 to £30,000. The miya-daiko is a double headed drum with thick cow hide nailed on either end with a double row of hefty tacks. Miya means 'temple' or 'shrine', while daiko means 'drum' (taiko when not linked to another qualifying word). The drum, like all Japanese drums, is renowned for its power to cleanse the air of evil spirits, and is therefore traditionally found in most temples. This drum is most recognisable to Westerners as the huge drum seen used by the Kodo drummers. The smaller drums can be stood on a wooden stand like a floor tom, while the larger ones are placed horizontally on hefty stands.

### SHIME-DAIKO (TIGHT/HIGH DRUM)

The shime-daiko is the equivalent of the Western snare drum, but without the snares (shime translating into 'tight', as in skin tension). Sizes can range from 13" to 14" in diameter and 6" deep. The solid shell is made from maple or cherrywood

and weighs approximately four kilos. Prices range from £2,000 upwards depending on how good the wood is and how elaborately the shell has been decorated by an artist; although not all shime-daikos are decorated. The two heads are made from thick cow skin and were once laced together with hemp rope — nowadays a mixture of cotton and nylon is used. The drum is pulled to tension just before a performance; this tensioning has even been made part of the Kodo ritual — each morning they form pairs and painstakingly pull the drums to tension, aided by the bashing of a huge stick. This drum dates back to the 8th century when it was used in the noh theatre, and later where it was used in popular kabuki music. The drum is supported on a small wooden stand on the floor with the player kneeling to play. Generally this drum is not used in gaga court music or in shrines.

### HIRA-DAIKO (SLENDER FRAMED DRUM)

This drum can range from 24" by 10" to almost 4' by 18", and can weigh anything from five to 30 kilos. The solid shell is made from Japanese elm or maple and has cow hide nailed in position on both sides. Like the shime-daiko, prices go from £2,000 upwards depending on the quality of the wood and the decoration.

This drum was primarily used in gagaku, royal court music, but not in the noh theatre (gagaku is derived from 'ga' — gentle/elegant — and 'gaku' — music). This drum is sometimes found in popular music and sometimes in shrines, although not as much as the miya daiko. Traditionally, this is a hanging drum and is suspended from a framework by metal rings.

### OKEDO (BARREL DRUM)

This drum is a rope-tensioned barrel drum and can vary in size from 16" by 18" to 6' by

✪ Miya-daiko (Temple drum)

✪ Shime-daiko (tight/high drum)

✪ Hira-daiko (slender framed drum)

✪ Odeko (barrel drum)

7'. The smaller ones can be held around the neck on a strap and can be played with two sticks, sometimes one on each end. This technique is noted as being more Korean than it is Japanese. The shell is much lighter that the miya daiko and is not made from one piece of wood but from slats, like a barrel. The larger drums are supported almost horizontally on a stand and are then played at one end only, or with a player at each end. This drum is primarily found in local folk music and popular music.

## CHAPA (SMALL CYMBALS)

Small brass cymbals varying in size from 7" to 10". Played in a similar manner to orchestral cymbals but with more of a time keeping function, there are a lot of techniques for this instrument, and it is sometimes used for soloing.

## KANE
## (OR SHOKO IN THE JAPANESE ORCHESTRA)

This popular time keeping device is made from blue bronze and played with a small beater, the head of which is made from water buffalo horn. The head of the beater is moved between the two opposite inside rims of the kane and sometimes on the inside surface. In the gagaku orchestra it is supported on a decorated stand and played with two beaters.

## STICKS

These can be an unbelievable four inches (yes, four inches) thick by 20" long. Typical sticks would be made from oak and would be 16" long, 2.5" thick and weigh approximately 200 grams each.

One peculiar stick sometimes found in Japan is a long thin stick not dissimilar to a headmaster's cane.

The thicker the stick, the more it is held in a fist like manner. The thinner the stick, the more the fulcrum is created between the thumb and first finger. Heavy playing is very important, so the fulcrum is never too dainty.

## JOJI HIROTA, HOKKAI DAIKO

Joji Hirota is without doubt one of the most innovative drummers one is ever likely to see. Steeped in the cultural tradition of North Japan, Joji studied Western classical percussion in Kyoto, the old capital of Japan, before setting off on a massive world tour with Stomu Yamashta and the Red Buddha Theatre.

He then settled in London (1972) and became Musical Director of the Lindsay Kemp Dance Company while juggling his remaining time to accommodate the fulfilment of a record deal in Japan and Britain, and regular visits for his training with the Japanese drumming group Hokkai Daiko, based in Nopboribetsu Hokkaido, North Japan. Under the parent-like guidance of master drummer Itto Oba, Joji found what he calls "the spiritual centre" of his drumming. These varying influences helped him develop his innovative and unusual drum setup, combining traditional Japanese drums, Western drum kit, Rototoms, cymbals, gongs, singing bowls, bells and bows — you name it.

Three solo albums later, Joji is still going strong. He has recorded for Real World with Trisan (featuring Guo Yue on Chinese flutes and Paul Breenon from Clannad on keyboards), as well as another album with Guo Yue on Riverboat records.

The future looks frightfully busy for Joji Hirota, but how did it all begin?

"When I was very little I used to play in local Autumn festivals in Hokkaido, North Japan. I used to feel very attracted to drumming and wanted to play drums, any drums."

What happened after that; did you study music at school?

"Yes. In Japanese schools you can't do Japanese drumming. I was lucky to be able

○ **Chapa (small cymbals)**

to do Western classical percussion, which was very important for me. After that I went on to Kyoto Art University and studied music. Even though I was not studying Japanese drumming at that time, it was something I felt deeply for."

So it was an important strand running through your life.

"I enjoyed it very much, but I found Japanese drumming more interesting when I came to Europe with the Red Buddha Theatre, a Japanese theatre company. We toured all over Europe and America. In England we played for six weeks at the Roundhouse; we did the Piccadilly Theatre and the ICA. That made me very interested in staying here, because the audiences responded so well and I got to know so many people. But then this made me want to go back to my roots, the music and percussion of my origin. I went back to Japan and approached one of the famous drumming groups of that period, Hokkai Daiko."

How did they react to you as someone who had studied Western percussion?

"First of all I telephoned the master's

son, and he said, 'Well you can't study just for a short period'. However, they knew I was a professional musician and let me go along to see how I got on."

Was it a very difficult introduction?

"It was very, very hard work. Six hours a day of extremely physical and exhausting work; such a different energy than I'd experienced before. I remember the drum sticks were so heavy, the drums were so hard to hit, and the work the whole body — particularly the arms and legs — had to do was unbelievable. Another thing was the huge blisters that would form all over your hands — I sometimes couldn't even turn the steering wheel of my car. I would secretly put plasters on my hands at the start of every day. Another thing was the concentration it all demanded; it was amazing. I thought sometimes I couldn't continue, but I knew I had to do it."

So it was stamina training as much as anything else?

"Yes, definitely, but also to find the correct posture and positions for arms, legs, hands and muscles in the playing technique."

Was this all happening at the same time that things were opening up in the UK for you?

"Yes, I became musical director for the Lindsay Kemp Dance Company, as well as being signed to a major label in Japan for a solo project. It was great working with Lindsay Kemp because he gave me total freedom to create my music. It was very good for me. I could incorporate any Japanese or Western influence I wanted. He would give me the basic ideas, what kind of moods, things were etc., but I pretty much had free reign after that."

Would you say he was a big influence on your playing and musical development at that time?

"Yes, because if you have freedom you can do so much, it puts such demands on you."

How long did that involvement continue?

"Three productions, but I wouldn't say it has finished. Maybe I'll do another one. Of course, during that time I was also releasing my solo albums as well."

Do you fell you've established a musical direction in that time and successfully integrated Eastern and Western percussion into your set up?

"Yes. I also studied other percussion — congas, bongos and Latin percussion. Not tabla or anything, but I studied a lot, drum kit as well. This all influenced my direction."

How do Japanese people respond to your setup, do they find it unusual?

"Most of the reactions I get are positive. It's generally a standard setup for me now, not different for each different piece of music, although I do adjust for some musical situations."

I've noticed that at the moment you've got the hanging bass drum (hira-daiko) on your left. Does it give you problems leading with your left hand, and how did it come about?

"Traditionally if there is only one drum then that should be played on the left of the player because then the right hand can hit with more strength. I'm right-handed, and I started off with the hira-daiko on my right

⊘ Kane (or shoko in the Japanese orchestra)

⊘ Joji Hirota, Hokkai Daiko

because of my setup of many drums. I changed for one show when it obscured me from the audience, and I never changed back. Now I always play with the drum in the traditional position. There are advantages — I feel that my left hand is purer at the moment, it produces a much clearer sound than the right on the hira-daiko."

What drummers and percussionists have been an influence on you?

"Weather Report drummers, particularly Omar Hakim. Also people like Zakir Hussain, Trilok Gurtu, and Morris Pert."

What about rock drummers? There's a similar physical energy there to that of Japanese drumming.

"Yes, but I'm more influenced by the dynamics and technique of tabla players and jazzier type drum kit players."

What's next?

"I'm writing a new album at the moment, using a lot more technology mixed with various percussion on top; a lot of classical influences, maybe some flute and things.

I am trying to aim for the future, a music

of the future. We have to work together — everybody. It doesn't matter whether you are Chinese, British or Japanese, we can work together, develop some kind of world music which relates people to one another.

At the same time, music in which you can find yourself and share that with others. But it just doesn't happen if two people are isolated from each other when they make music.

# chapter 5
## Shut Up!

Tone, timbre and touch. The three 'T's — crucial ingredients in the recipe of instruments that make up your drum kit, financial restraints aside. How you tune your toms, what sort of cymbals you're using, how much cut you need, whether you're going through a PA... These are things that every drummer has to contend with, aside from the obligatory tricky business of technique. However, drummers are known throughout the music world as being noisy. Loud. And the thing is, there's a lot of truth to this; most of us play loud, and at gigs even louder. It's exciting, you can't deny it — the adrenaline takes hold and even the most level headed tai-chi types among us start to hit a little harder. As a result, I for one end up hearing my kit rather than listening to it; a problem made worse by the fact that you don't want to damage your hearing, and no matter how effective they are, you can't truly appreciate the subtleties of your kit with ear plugs in, regardless of how much acclimatising you do. Apart from an almost inevitable loss of control, playing loud has one principle disadvantage: the infinite subtleties of the drums and cymbals in front of you can be lost forever; timbre and touch can go out of the window.

If you play loud, amplified music, the chances of getting heard rather than listened to are slight, and in the confusion things can get louder and louder. While loud music can set you off a treat, sometimes it's so loud on stage that things get unlistenable, although they're all too audible. Suddenly, all the questions you may have asked yourself about your sound, your style, are wiped out. For example, if, like me, you buy cymbals that are smaller because they're cheaper, and as a result are quite used to having an immediate and 'poppy' sound to your crashes — you hit them, they go away — when you finally get enough dough together for a large crash, it's arrival is absolutely terrifying. Suddenly you have a cymbal that won't go away; a crash that you can hit quietly with real confidence; a cymbal that puts in an unimaginable amount of bottom end. The whole sound picture (that's a picture, like, of sound, man) is turned on its head. But then, when you play loud, the chances are this is all irrelevant, and it means that we could be forgetting how to listen. So where can we re-learn how to listen?

The other night, an idle hour in hand, I watched *How Do They Do That?* — a programme which chiefly raises the question, "Why Do I Watch This?" Apart from the usual rubbish along the lines of how they made the pigs talk in Babe (guess what — with a computer! It's not just drummers they're replacing with machines, it's piglets too!), in amongst the adverts for adverts, there was a fascinating piece about Evelyn Glennie, in which she explained how she had developed her appreciation for and understanding of different sounds and textures, despite being deaf. Now, before I go any further, this is not the reason that Evelyn is such an interesting percussionist and general mega-star. The fact is, she is a phenomenal player with awe-inspiring talent and technique — her records would teach anyone a thing or two. She's forthright in her opinions — I'll never forget the masterclass she gave where she commented that drum kit players tend to play too loud, and that she had told Billy Cobham just that. But what she had to say about technique and understanding sounds in terms of their relative frequency, how she first learnt to differentiate between various drum sounds by feeling them through her body, was very thought provoking and set my mind racing.

Although she is a 'classical' musician, Glennie offered a fresh perspective on the dilemma we can all face; what she has learnt to do is listen — I mean that in the profoundest sense — even though she can't hear. Taking advantage of the fact that percussion is so physically immediate — you hit the thing, that's it, there's the sound — Evelyn talks about feeling the sound of the toms she plays in her face; and about gauging the pitch of the notes she plays on the tuned instruments by how far the

frequencies travel up her hands, the higher notes getting as far as her little finger, the lower all the way up her middle finger. Sometimes, in order to sense exactly what tone she is getting out of an instrument, Glennie will let the stick move into a different grip, to see how it's responding to the way she's striking the drum. Such application, such technique renders most of us unthinking Neanderthal beasts by comparison.

So I got to thinking that maybe belting seven bells out of everything isn't the best way forward — especially if I'm being monitored. The last gig I played with wedges I found myself playing quieter and quieter — because it was so loud coming out of the wedge — and my whole sound changed. Now, while I'd prefer to have everything, the whole band, quieter so the sound of my kit was more 'true', the whole process was very stimulating; and because I was playing with considerably more control, the drums spoke in a different way. So what I suggest is that we all spend ten minutes every day playing very, very quietly — just tapping snare drums all over, rather than rim-shotting furiously; feeling the drums move and breathe; striking the edges of the cymbals with the shoulder of the stick (an old jazz trick, admittedly, but don't let that put you off). That way we could all experience some of those musical grey areas that could make life pretty interesting. So give it a go — try playing quieter and rediscover the three 'T's. There's another plus, too: you won't annoy your neighbours half as much. But then again, where's the fun in that?

# chapter 6
## Body Talk

### The Hearing Aid

Loss of hearing has always been something of a worry for musicians, though drummers tend to take it less seriously than most, partly because we don't need to pitch accurately in order to play our instruments, and partly because of our intrinsic masochism. Rather, it's our loved ones who fret that banging and crashing about will do irreparable damage to our ears (and theirs). There's no doubt that excessive noise affects hearing profoundly, and that rock musicians are beginning to suffer from hearing disorders like tinnitus (a persistent ringing in the ears), loudness discomfort, and of course, partial deafness (an inability to hear certain frequencies).

Technically, the ear is divided into three sections: external, middle and inner. The first part is the bit you see most of; beautifully designed and shaped to receive low frequency, high intensity noise like drumming, and to pinpoint exactly where and sound is coming from. That sound is then funnelled into the middle ear itself via a tube which has the actual eardrum set at an angle across its inner end. Behind this is the middle ear cavity which is spanned by three small bones: the hammer, anvil and stirrup.

So, a sound passes through the ear canal on its way to the drum, which is the membrane that causes those three tiny bones in the middle ear to move in the rhythm of the sound. This in turn persuades a fluid in the inner ear to move sympathetically, along with the tiny hair cells of various lengths bathed within. These cells transform that movement into nerve impulses which are carried to the brain and interpreted as sound. It's these cells which are attacked, stunned, and sometimes killed by loud noises. I should point out here that the actual definition of 'noise' is simply any unwanted sound. So our long suffering parents were right when they asked us to stop that bloody noise!

Now, a word on ear-wax. Ear-wax is actually not as nasty a substance as it seems. It's secreted by the skin of the canal and humidifies, moisturises and even acts as an antiseptic to the ear. It also catches particles of dust and other rubbish that might find their way into the ear, thereby preventing damage to the actual eardrum.

Of course, the ear is not just responsible for hearing; it's also responsible for balance. This is why extremely loud or unexpected noises can make you feel like you're falling down a hole. I'm reliably informed by experts that if music does this to you, it's definitely way too loud.

I once worked in Germany, demonstrating drums at a trade show, and after one of my clinics was accosted by a very serious teutonic lady in a white lab coat. She suggested that, if I always played drums that loudly, I surely must be deaf by now. I was tempted to put my hand to my ear and ask her to speak up. I didn't though, and when it turned out that the German government were seriously worried about musicians' hearing loss and were actually testing them there and then, I decided to give it a go. She sat me down, gave me some headphones and proceeded to feed me what appeared to be random high and low frequency tones. I simply responded my nodding my head to every sound I could hear. I wasn't able to cheat because she sat behind a screen and I couldn't see her moving the frequency control, but I actually astonished her (and myself) by being able to clearly hear all the frequencies that 'normal' people could.

I guess I've been lucky, because during my career I've been exposed to an awful lot of noise, although I've always tried to place myself out of danger wherever possible. This might have given rise to my back problems, as in the past I've been forced to twist my head and upper body unnaturally away from some excruciatingly loud amplifiers.

More years ago than I care to count, bands used to go to Germany to 'get it together', and often ended up playing up to nine 45-minute spots a night on a small club stage. This was roughly the time when music was becoming more aggressive and progressive (q.v. louder), and within a short time we musicians would collectively suffer from what was known as 'the blanket'. This wasn't just high-end loss, because, in fact, all the frequencies became muddied, a bit like playing with a blanket over your head. It wasn't a permanent affliction, and the next day all was, ostensibly, back to normal. Or was it? I paid a visit to London's famous Royal National Throat, Nose and Ear Hospital, where Dr Barbara Cadge, an eminent hearing specialist, told me a great deal about degrees of hearing loss at certain frequencies.

Unfortunately, there's really no yardstick dictating the amount of time you can actually listen to loud noise without impairing your hearing, because some evidently have 'soft' ears while others have 'hard'. Certainly, people in industry are not allowed to subject themselves to average sound levels of 90dB(A) without wearing hearing protectors, but so far there is no specific legislation for musicians, or even their audiences. However, the government's Health and Safety Executive have produced proposals aimed at reducing the risk to workers (including musicians) and members of the public at gigs. These state that:

**1.** *Delay towers should be used to distribute sound around a venue and therefore reduce the exposure of the audience to high sound levels. (The implication being that if you only have PA speakers at each side of the stage, these have to be very loud to reach the back of the hall, thereby deafening the people in the front few rows.)*

**2.** *Sound levels should not exceed 104dB(A) in any public area.*

**3.** *If sound levels are likely to exceed 96dB(A), promoters should ensure that information concerning potential hearing risks is given to the audience.*

Of course, all of this is good for the audience, but I'm not sure if this prospective legislation will really help the poor musician. Since all laws and health guidelines refer to sound levels in decibels, I once conducted a test monitoring the levels put out by the instruments around the drummer (including his own) to build up a better picture. Note that the decibel scale is a logarithmic one, where an increase of 3dB results in a sound which is twice as loud (ie. 98dB is twice as loud as 95dB).

I placed an IVIE audio analyser (which meters the peaks of sound) at roughly my ear level, and played as loudly as usual with the following results. An 8″ wooden snare drum put out 140dB, while a metal piccolo was measured at 141dB. Even an 18″ bass drum achieved a creditable 127dB, while a 16″ crash at 134dB was exactly twice as loud as a 21″ Earth ride at 131dB. The quietest element of the kit was a pair of 12″ hi-hats which managed 124dB. Putting these findings into context, a power chord through a Fender Twin with the analyser at ear level in front of it registered 125dB; and it's estimated that this same chord would have been in excess of 130dB through a Marshall stack (the same sound level would be recorded by a bass, which needs to be considerably louder to be audible).

On balance, these levels appear to be worryingly excessive, but with sound the danger is exacerbated by its duration. After all, a snare drum hit invariably lasts for under a second, while even a slow crash cymbal won't sustain for much more than five seconds. No, it's obviously the instruments which sustain high levels for a long time (like guitars and

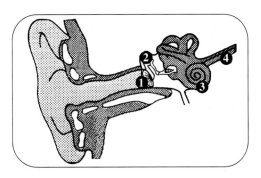

✪ 1. Eardrum converts sound to vibration. 2. Three small bones carry vibrations to fluid in the inner ear. 3. Cochlea changes vibrations into electrical impulses. 4. Nerves carry impulses to brain.

keyboards) which we should avoid being too near. That said, drums are inherently loud instruments on impact. In the 1970s, Leeds Town Hall employed a device called a Decibelometer which switched off the power to the equipment as soon as certain sound levels were exceeded. It was a laudable attempt to protect the audience, but it was set at far too low a threshold for rock music, something like 90dB(A), and even unamplified drums could trip the meter with hilarious consequences. Incidentally, the ear is not particularly fussy about which sort of sound frequencies cause it to malfunction, but in what specialists call 'leisure hearing', it's the frequencies between 3 and 6 kHz which are invariably lost due to noise. It seems the heavy bass end is just as culpable in wreaking havoc with our hearing as the screaming guitar or organ. And even though our ability to hear high frequencies does diminish somewhat with age and noise bombardment, the others don't. I asked Dr Cadge if musicians were more prone to hearing loss than others, since they might be said to use their ears more. Her immediate answer was that, in a healthy person who wasn't abusing his or her ears, it shouldn't matter. The same held true for older people, whose ears, providing there was no evidence of diseases like diabetes, high blood pressure or even high cholesterol levels, were no more vulnerable than a youngster's.

So if, as I said, my hearing's intact after all the years I've been playing, have I just been lucky? Well, yes and no. Strange as it may seem, there's a school of thought which says that people like me, with dark hair and dark eyes, have better resistance to noise than those with blonde hair and blue eyes. And as I've already said, I've always tried to keep well away from loud noises. It's much better to be sitting slightly back from the other guy's amplifiers in a concert situation, and out of line with them in all others. There was a hippie guy known as Jesus, who habitually used to stand in the bass bins of the PA system at the old Roundhouse in the 1970s. History hasn't recorded exactly what long term affect this had on his hearing or even whether he was a natural blonde, but I expect he was seeing God at the time anyway.

Headphones can be a very real danger to musicians, and the modern drummer tends to be the most vulnerable because of the dreaded click track. In an effort to hang on to it like grim death, we tend to turn it up louder and louder, and are seriously in danger of momentarily deafening ourselves. I once wandered into the studio after a playback and heard my cans playing back from something like 30 feet. I was appalled by how loud they were; they were more like sibilant hi-fi speakers. Measured in decibels, I don't suppose they were quite at what's known technically as 'the threshold of pain' (140dB), but they were bloody loud. Funnily enough, Dr Cadge assured me that headphones aren't dangerous per se; it's the sound levels themselves that hurt your ears.

There are a couple of famous drummers who, rumour has it, suffer from impaired hearing. Willie Green with the Neville Brothers (who I wouldn't consider to be an excessively loud band) allegedly blasted his eardrum during a soundcheck — something which normally takes the force of an explosion to initiate. And Terry Bozzio is said to suffer from high end loss, and is resorting to very specialised ear mufflers which are custom made for his ears alone.

Until now, I've never been one for those tuned ear defenders, since they tend to attenuate the high frequencies and distort the musical spectrum, or take too much of the sound quality away and muffle it to the extent that it changes the way I dynamically respond to it. But having tested a sample recently, I'm slowly coming round. The ones I tried are called Ultra Tech ER20 and are made in the US. They provide a tuned acoustic network comprising a filter and precision manufactured ducting, are made in three pieces, and simply cut out some of the music without distorting it. Gun shops also sell protectors called North Sonic II for a tenner or so, which I'm told are the business because they're designed to reduce only peaks of sound, like those produced by explosions. I have seen the type Terry Bozzio uses advertised; they're also American-built and cut down across the whole frequency range. A company called Etymotic Research make them, and they can cost up to $150 simply because they have to be moulded to your very own canal. So unless you're actually in America, they'd be nigh impossible to get. However, I understand from Dr Cadge that in extreme cases this sort of protection can be available here too, although she points out that it can be uncomfortable.

But what about those squashy yellow ones you get in your local chemist, or even good old-fashioned cotton wool? Well, the experts of the medical profession take the view that anything which affords some degree of defence is better than nothing, even screwed up pieces of loo paper. But since hearing loss is irreversible, it's in musicians' own interests to protect their hearing properly.

I've always suspected that my ears had a built-in defence mechanism which allowed me to hit hard without discomfort, simply because I could anticipate the sound. You may have noticed when someone hits a drum loudly next to you, it only really hurts if you're not expecting it. Dr Cadge corroborated my thoughts on this and told me that the phenomenon is known as Temporary Threshold Shift, and is nature's way of stopping us deafening ourselves. She went on to say that the middle ear has a tiny muscle within that reacts to loud sound and serves to partially dislocate the chain and protect the inner ear. It won't wear out and will work as long as there's no injury from disease. There's even a damper in the middle ear which comes in at 85-95dB(A) and which, there's even some evidence to say, can be triggered before the sound. But beware, this is not grounds for bombarding your ears and hoping all the various failsafes will protect you. Temporary Threshold Shift can easily become Permanent Threshold Shift.

So there are things we drummers can do to protect our hearing, even though, like keyboard players, we're static and unable to move out of the way of the loudest noises with ease. And we all know how hard it is to get a guitarist to turn down (the old joke has it that putting the music in front of him helps). More intelligent drum set positioning is one option, and you could always turn the offending amplifier away from you a little. Use hearing protectors, and remember that with noise damage there's a direct relationship between intensity of noise and duration. So allow your ears to rest every so often when recording.

There was a wonderful programme on TV which showed Evelyn Glennie in Brazil, taking part in a samba school and marching in the Mardi Gras parade. She held her own very well, so much so that one began to suspect that the problems with her hearing couldn't be that bad. However, by a miracle of science the BBC were able to show us just how little Evelyn could hear. It was astonishing because she seemed to be able to hear music as if it were being played at minimal volume next door, just about penetrating the walls.

It's difficult to say what constitutes a loud band because of measuring difficulties; even the Health and Safety Executive recognise that where you measure the noise makes a hell of a difference. But it's felt that bands who exceed 120dB for any length of time are at a critically high level. For safety reasons *The Guinness Book Of Records* no longer lists superlatives of loudness, but The Who used to hold the record at 120dB(A), while in 1987 an American band called Immaculate Mary were measured at 123dB(A) from 50 metres away. Mind you, any band would need to work really hard to emulate a jet aircraft which puts out 140dB(A) on take off.

An audiogram, which is the traditional yardstick for hearing loss, only measures from 0.25Hz to 8kHz, and musicians need to hear clearly frequencies much further up the scale than that. Dr Cadge says musicians will frequently report hearing difficulties at the high end, way above the 8kHz ceiling where an audiogram would be able to spot the problem.

Can we get our hearing tested on the National Health? Yes, but only if we can persuade our GP that we have a real problem, whereupon he'll ultimately refer us to a specialist. I can't recommend that anyone clog up the NHS by feigning hearing loss, but if you simply want to reassure yourself, you could go privately to a specialist for a consultation and an audiogram that'll put you back roughly £65. Ring your local hospital and they'll no doubt give you the relevant information.

In conclusion, a word of warning: EXCESSIVE EXPOSURE TO LOUD MUSIC CAN CAUSE PERMANENT HEARING DAMAGE. As Dr Cadge told me, there's only one real marker as to whether noise has damaged your hearing, and that's after it's happened. Once the threshold has been shifted down as a response to noise, it can't be predicted how many times the ear can recover from being exposed to the same noise again and again.

## You Need Hands

Hands up any drummer who has never had any trouble with his hands. I'm not talking about the carpal tunnel syndrome which poor old Carl Palmer has been afflicted with and is now thankfully cured of; no, what I mean is those day-to-day cuts, blisters and abrasions which tend to appear at the wrong time.

For more years than I'm prepared to admit I simply put up with blisters coming up on my forefingers and, more especially, since I use the orthodox grip, the pad on my left hand between my thumb and index finger. This is where the stick bounces and is frequently missing several layers of skin. Incidentally, there are five layers of skin on the human body, then tissue below them, and finally flesh and bone. All this bloody mess was inconvenient and painful until 1984 when I discovered the joys of prophylactics and safe drumming. Like most drummers I'd

wait until there was a series of holes in my hand with bone about to stick through, whereupon I'd do my best to mend or at least protect my poor hands with sticking-plaster, bandages, or worse still Nu-skin. I know we drummers are masochists, but the agony inherent in applying that perfectly sterile and otherwise innocuous product to an open wound gives a completely new slant to the phrase 'no pain, no gain'.

Anyway I got smart, and began applying a piece of woven and therefore spongy sticking plaster to my hands before I began to play and the damage was done. Lateral thinking or what? It worked, although to give complete protection I find it needs to be applied quite some time before the gig, and since the flesh below has still taken a hammering, it needs to be taken off with great care. The stuff I use is flesh-coloured, 2″ wide, and with a thin pink stripe in the middle — it's made by Johnson & Johnson in America. Although I'm told you can get it over here, I've never seen it, but I expect some equivalent must be available.

This constant battering of the hands has concerned me ever since a doctor in America treating me for bronchitis, looked at my calluses, and gave me the completely unsolicited advice that while he didn't feel they were carcinogenic, they could be. As if we drummers didn't have enough problems finding the right sticks and heads to use. The Doc, who was incidentally wearing Nike trainers, Levis and a Grateful Dead T-shirt, went on to freak me out by informing me that a cancer cell could be created as a result of constantly repeated trauma — a bit like the sort of thing we drummers do from time to time, and which the surviving players of my generation have been doing for two thirds of their life! I checked this worrying information out with another doctor who put my mind at rest.

He maintained that if there was already a cancerous cell in evidence then any form of irritation, be it mechanical or otherwise, would serve to stimulate its growth. But the hammering we drummers do to our hands, whilst it may well abrade the skin, is not going to create anything untoward. That said, Dr. Drum considers our hands to be a very unusual place to find a cancer in the first place.

I have to admit I'm not the sort of drummer who has felt the need for drummer's gloves — although there have been times when I've wished I had a magic pair to take the pain away after a long tour. Although I can't help feeling that they're a bit like having a bath with your boots on, I certainly wouldn't look down on anyone who owned a pair. Unless I've missed something, drum gloves come in two different types: with fingers or without; and there don't seem to be quite so many manufacturers making them anymore. Certainly Zildjian, Vic Firth and so on are still making them from leather, and they all appear to be up around the £20 mark. But I'm told by an otherwise completely reliable source that there are rubber sheaths available these days which simply slip onto the stick and cushion the impact.

There is no substitute for practice to harden your hands, but if all else fails, you might like to try something which was recommended to me to toughen mine up when I first began playing. It was suggested that I rub urine on them. I can't actually remember whether it was my own or someone else's in question, but it was certainly a serious recommendation. I know we drummers are capable of accidentally peeing on our hands in crowded toilets at gigs, but to stand in the queue and do it intentionally before the gig seems to me to be taking the remedy to its illogical conclusion. I spoke to the aforementioned doctor and he didn't dismiss the idea at all. It seems that besides people like Ali Bhuto and Sarah Miles drinking the stuff for their own well being (although not necessarily for the well-being of anybody watching), older people actually apply it to pertinent parts of their bodies as a defence against rheumatism — they've even been known to bathe their feet in a bowl of it. However, there's no scientific evidence that it does any good except as a placebo. But the sympathetic MD tells me that since urine is an acid of sorts, it definitely would toughen up the skin. Even so, it might be a safer idea to try this out on a day when you haven't been out for a chicken vindaloo washed down with a few pints of lager the night before.

## The Body Beautiful

Conservation of energy... now there's a thing. It's a term that's normally associated with industry and heating bills, but it can also be a very important aspect of successful live drumming.

There's a strange, compelling sensation that all musicians experience just prior to stepping up onto a stage; it's that mind-focusing, heart-warming glow... called nausea. Everybody endures it in varying degrees, and although it can never be completely removed, there are a tremendous number of things that can be done to help alleviate its incapacitating effects.

Nausea (a dicey subject at the best of times) is brought on by the knowledge that only minutes now separate you from an impatient, beat-hungry audience, and that your drumming ability, your music, and even your dress (if you wear one) will be exposed to unbridled criticism and scrutiny. While elsewhere in this book you'll find advice on gaining confidence, organising yourself to play live, and stage fright, here we're going to deal with some of the other, more fundamental topics.

## PUMPING HICKORY

The first is fitness (yes, your fitness). In terms of energy expended, a gig can be something of a monumental occasion for a drummer. As you can tell from the blisters and your inability to breathe afterwards, the effort made during your performance is many, many times greater than that made at rehearsals or back in the bedroom (drumming, that is). As a result, your body has to be physically capable not only of enduring the pre-performance stress and nausea, but also of maintaining the same level of strenuous application and enthusiasm throughout the set.

Drummers, more so than any other type of musician, cannot afford to have their energy peter out towards the end of a gig, and should therefore consider it an essential part of their preparation to be training for stamina, endurance and strength — particularly the strength of their wrists, forearms, shoulders and ankles.

Running and swimming are by far the best private activities to indulge in if you want to build stamina. Neither require large quantities of cash or equipment, and, though not normally looked upon as an integral part of the drummer's routine, can do nothing but good for your performance. There are few really top stick-wielders who are not also concerned about their fitness. Stewart Copeland runs everywhere; Billy Cobham does 400 sit-ups every day; and Neil Peart spends as much time sitting on his bike as he does at his kit. Though they may do all this for fun, the likelihood is that they have learnt to prepare physically for a gig in much the same way as a boxer prepares for a fight

— twelve rounds, twelve numbers; each requiring the same degree of application.

Aside from running and/or swimming (the latter is obviously going to improve your stamina and the strength of your upper body), a pair of comparatively inexpensive dumbbells are all that you really need to specifically strengthen wrists, forearms and shoulders. Volume upon volume has been written about basic weight-training, so finding a cheap, comprehensive guide to the actual exercises for each body part (as we say in the fitness business) should be easy. The main thing is that you give the idea some serious consideration and look upon it not as a thankless chore, but as an easy way of doing yourself a big, big favour.

## ALL THINGS IN MODERATION

Now let's talk about alcohol. In particular, the effect it will have on your performance. The majority of drummers find themselves torn between either 'getting a few in' before the gig in an attempt to replace all that rapidly dissipating courage, or sticking to the ol' orange juice until after the show. Well, the facts are simple. While alcohol will, for most, have a temporary, pick-me-up-and-take-me-to-it effect, the dividing line between having just enough to pep you up and having just enough to slow you down is very fine indeed, especially when you're not at your most rational, ie. immediately before a gig. If you really can strike a balance and you know how much is too much, all well and good; otherwise, steer clear altogether.

Another myth that's worth dissolving is this business about pumping your body full of chocolate and other sticky, sugary things to fire yourself with temporary energy. With the exception of fruit (which for anyone about to expend energy is all good news, and the more the better), any foodstuff that contains a high percentage/overall quantity of refined sugar (chocolate, cakes, canned drinks etc.) will promote an initial, short-lived surge in energy followed, usually somewhere around the middle of the gig, by a rapid drain, as your body tries to counter the resulting increase in blood sugar by drawing on the muscles' energy reserves — reserves you were hoping to be able to use for the latter half of the gig.

Just remember, Dutch courage and a Mars a day are alright in extreme moderation, but the self-confidence you'll promote by eating and drinking more sensibly on the night will be far more lasting and supportive if you really care about more than just the opening number.

### HINTS FOR THE PERSPIRING ARTIST

Now, sweat. Sweat and gravity. Both are amongst the drummer's worst enemies and work cunningly together to provide some of the most soul-destroying, infuriating, or just plain embarrassing moments you'll ever endure on stage.

Two things about sweat. Firstly, it causes sight problems. When the 'big sting' hits your eyes, it leads to distraction and a loss of much needed concentration. Secondly, sticks, by the nature of their design, enjoy no greater pastime than to fly dramatically from your grip at the first coming-together of effort and perspiration.

Many people are anti-wristband and vehemently anti-headband, which is fair enough if sweating is only a very minor problem. The majority of drummers are, however, constantly at the mercy of sliding sticks and poor visibility, and so should bear in mind that their audience will forget the wearing of the headband sooner than the spectacular losing of sticks.

Another handy hint for the profusely damp amongst you, is to always have a dispenser of those pre-moistened (sometimes antiseptic) wipes standing next to your carton of sugar-free orange juice. In between each number, a quick wipe-over of your face, forearms and hands with these before you dry off on your clean towel will remove — rather than simply redistribute — all the greasiness that causes the problems (including Acne Rosea Postus Gigus).

### WEARING IT OUT ON THE STAGE

Everyone has their own ideas about what to wear on stage. Obviously, your fellow musicians' garb is going to influence your decision as much as anything, but certain other things should be taken into account as well.

Tight jeans are really a no-no for enthusiastic drummers (and, indeed, everyone else). Although you may think they look good 'n' sexy as you step up from the throng and take your position, firstly, they don't, and secondly, by the end of the first number only you know you've still got them on (and boy, will you know). Much better to aim for looser, lighter clothes — beltless trousers, lightweight shoes that allow your feet to breathe, and the avoidance of all things nylon or otherwise man-made to prevent unnecessary overheating (again, in the interests of energy conservation).

Another important thing about clothes, is that you should take them with you separately to the gig. Don't wear them all evening; use the last half hour before you clamber up on stage to prepare yourself in all respects. Take time out to warn your body what is to be expected of it in the next couple of hours by warming up, limbering up, and psyching yourself up to be able to cope.

By the time you reach the stage, you want to be ready; you want to be able to hit the stage running. If you've eaten fairly sensibly, kept your alcohol intake to a minimum, and chosen clothing that will be doing you a favour rather than just blindly following fashion, the evening will end up a far more rewarding one for you and, hopefully, your audience.

Drumming is a physically demanding pastime; keep off the beer and stay in tune.

# chapter 7
## Vocal Exercises

Which drummers do you like and, more to the point, why do you like them? Is it because they can execute super-fast inverted flam-paradiddles around their monstrous kit without even picking up a pair of sticks? Or is it because they just play the way they do, something indefinable? Do you like the artistry that they employ, the style, the 'it' they have; or is it simply a matter of learned behaviour, reflexology? Is drumming an art, necessarily grounded in technique, or is it simply a skill, like plumbing? Are drummers painters, or are they plumbers? Well I'm ready to bet my bottom dollar that it's the indefinable, the 'something' that you can't quite put your finger on. More than that, I'll say right here and now that the most important thing you can do when learning to play the drums is not to study independence, time keeping or shining up your cymbals (though that's a very close second). No, the most important thing you can do is find your own voice. Your own voice? What does he mean? It's simple really; if you want to express yourself through music — and I can understand that you might want to earn a living instead — then you have got to bring that indefinable you to what you're doing.

Okay, an example — I'm resorting to Ringo Starr again as my case for the defence. Now, there are all sorts of reasons why Ringo played the way he did. He was left-handed playing a right-handed kit, meaning he came off around the kit leading with his left, meaning that his back beat was more emphatic than most of his contemporaries. He was coming straight out of a mutant rock 'n' roll cabaret culture, not just playing in strip clubs in Hamburg, but also in Butlins (same difference?), a job he quit for the Beatles. These are all obviously factors that shaped his style. But to understand exactly why, when — as many would assert — he was no great shakes, The Beatles took him on when the big time beckoned, all you have to do is listen to the *Anthology* record of out-takes and odds and sods. Ringo just has 'it'. In spades. His effect on the band is amazing; they change up a whole gear. This 'it' has inspired whole legions of American drummers, and, on a smaller scale, is solace to me. If he could do it, then so could I, I think on my darker paradiddling days.

Other drummers who have their voice are plentiful nowadays, although often enough you find that those with the most distinctive voices are those with the biggest overdrafts. As David Garibaldi once said, "Play dumb — you don't get paid for being smart." Not that having a voice is necessarily synonymous with having top notch chops, oh no.

And there, you see, is the can of worms I have been trying to tip-toe around, and I've just been and gone and opened it. Yes, chops Vs feel — something that I am facing up to right now, because after years of self-taught bluff, bluster and general bullshittery, I have finally got on with working on practising harder at playing the drums. I've started from the bottom up, working on my rudiments with the help of the written works of (amongst others) Buddy Rich and Ian Palmer. This is because I can't practise in the new flat I've moved into unless it's on my knee or a practice pad, and because I can't sit in front of the TV all day. I mean, I can, but you've got to do something with your hands — quiet at the back there.

When it comes to playing, my experience is largely in bands where we do 'our' thing. I can hold my own, and do actually have 'my way' of doing things — a sort of bustling but nevertheless big-beated clatter, that's my thing. Besides, I find that when I'm playing, my rudiments run at about 50 percent of practice pad skill; sometimes there just isn't time to play that tricky figure you've been cracking all week. Now I'm not saying don't practise, of course not, the opposite in fact. I mean that if you follow the idea that your overall playing is a voice, surely the bigger the vocabulary, the better you are at speaking. Well not necessarily; how many people do you know who can talk plenty but don't really have anything to say? So having all these 'words' at your disposal is no use unless you know how to use them. And the only way to do

that is to play with other people or listen a lot — to everything! A tall order perhaps, but as Steve Smith always says, unless we look into where the music came from and the drum kit's heritage, the chances are we'll be cut off from our roots. I am not advocating a Year Zero return to Elvis and Ringo, but that it is their vocabulary that we are essentially drawing on. Anyone — me even — can play like Dave Weckl if they learn hard enough, but they'll never know why he does what he does the way he does, if that is all that they have set out to do.

All this became clear to me when I attended (after a fashion) *Rhythm Live* 1995, where the talents of *Rhythm*'s writers were placed under public scrutiny. Peter Lockett, a master craftsman if ever there was one, and a man truly at one with his instrument. Mark Roberts, whose awesome state of the art melding of sampling and acoustic funky drumming left many jaws of the floor. And rock Hercules Simon Hanson — this man wields a righteous stick and pumps a fulsome pedal. Backstage before the show, I got chatting with those present. Blokeish modesty abounded, and everyone went on about how ropy their chops were, and how, y'know, don't expect anything too flash. I nodded enthusiastically; 'No', I was saying, 'don't expect too much from me'. Then, of course, the assembled crew delivered and awe-inspiring display of not just chops but (and this is the important bit) of personality.

The aforementioned each have a voice. It's them playing, no one else. And as a result, for the first time ever at a drum clinic I didn't feel the urge to take a chainsaw to my drums and give up forever. Because, humble as my chops are, I think I play the drums the way I do, not the way anyone else does, and they can't take that away from me.

# chapter 8
## Tactics

### About Time

In the live playing situation, the initiation of most tunes is left in the skilful hands of the drummer. He or she is endowed with a single bar stick striking solo in order to shove off each song into its speedy or sluggish safari of musical perambulation. With this responsibility the drummer must precisely evaluate the correct speed of the imminent song in order to clearly and confidently communicate the tempo to the other members of the ensemble. This confidence can only be displayed if the drummer blatantly and convincingly knows the correct tempo and feel. It is always vital that the drummer's account of the speed is the official and only pace to be employed, otherwise the song may resemble the Catcliffe and Treaton Working Men's Club summer outing — both requiring several bars to settle down.

The human brain with which we are all equipped has many amazing facets. It is perfectly capable of learning specific song tempos and feels, just like it can recall the exact gap between songs on a tape after repeated listening, and remember the exact running order of tracks on an album, even after years of not hearing it.

If you know a song inside out, remembering the tempo is natural and easy, so if you can find a way of acquainting yourself with the natural ability of recalling individual tempos, it could be very useful.

To some people this poses no problem as they can feel accurately many different tempos and select a speed as if it were logged permanently in their head. Others have to find a way of forcing this ability through learning tempos and finding methods of triggering the brain to recall what it has remembered.

My starting point for achieving this ability is to find three reference points across the velocity spectrum. Most modern music falls between 60 and 140 beats per minute (bpm), so my points of reference fall at 60, 100 and 140 bpm, giving me a fairly rough divide of all the tempos I might use.

60 bpm is of course one beat per second, so this, my first tempo, is quite easy to store. Remembering how long a second lasts should be no problem. As a child I was always told that a second should last the same amount of time as a four syllable word; so if you count 'one rhinoceros, two rhinoceros etc.', then as long as each word is spoken naturally and not rushed, your count

○ **Digital, analogue and mechanical bpm**

should be around 60 bpm. Once you have mastered this, halving it will, of course give you 120 bpm.

My next port of call is at 100 bpm. To remember this tempo I employ a method that I find never fails. At 100 bpm I can comfortably play a 16 beat pattern (semi-quavers) with just my right hand, so if I beat out this pattern on my knee to the fastest comfortable speed, I know I'm at 100 bpm. If I need a tempo around 100, I just adjust up or down accordingly. The same method applies to 140 bpm — at this speed my right hand can comfortably execute eight loud beats of semi-quavers. This is also my top speed for two-handed shuffles.

The only problem with this method is that as you progress as a player, your speed and agility increase. When I first put this method into practice, my single handed sixteens were at about 90 bpm, so one has to

constantly monitor and adjust.

Remember these ideas are only a rough guide to song speeds. The methods I use relate purely to my own physical limits. You will have to experiment with your own playing quirks to find the tempos you need. A short time with a metronome should give you some ideas.

Another sometimes more accurate method for tempo recall is having a selection of well known songs logged into you brain with their respective tempos and feels. For example, I know from memory that the Led Zeppelin track 'Good Times, Bad Times' was recorded at 94 bpm and has a straight four feel. So if I need to play at 94 bpm in straight 4/4, I think of that good old track and am instantly provided with a speed and feel. Many of the songs I have mentally logged are songs I have recorded or have had to play many times, so the vital information is clearly imprinted on my brain. I can still clearly recite the tempo of the first record I ever played on: it was 123 bpm and is as clear to me today as it was when I performed on it 17 years ago.

Here's a list of a few classic tracks that span the tempo spectrum:

| | | |
|---|---|---|
| Eagles | *'Hotel California'* | 74 bpm |
| Queen | *'We Will Rock You'* | 80 bpm |
| Beatles | *'We Can Work It Out'* | 105 bpm |
| Deep Purple | *'Smoke On The Water'* | 115 bpm |
| Beatles | *'Ticket To Ride'* | 125 bpm |
| Motorhead | *'Ace Of Spades'* | 144 bpm |

These ideas in no way replace the metronome or offer any degree of total accuracy. Most music software today offers tempo adjustment to .00 of a bpm, and you would have to be very clever to offer that accuracy, let alone confidently say, "That's 82.43 bpm boys — honest."

This is all just theory that I've found very useful, even though I always carry a metronome — you would be surprised how often the battery is flat or it's too dark to read the dial. As drummers we need to take a bit of responsibility in knowing our tempos, as we are always getting it in the neck because we don't actually produce a tonal note — this really is one in the eye for the musical snobs.

# Head Masterclass

Judging by the amount of enquiries I get, and from the questions on the letters pages of percussion magazines, tuning a set of drums seems to be the one problem that unites the most disparate players. How do you do it, and how can you improve upon it when you think you already can? I'd like to share some observations and tips with you, and offer a little help, but before I do, I feel I ought to make some kind of disclaimer.

This is not because I don't have confidence in what I'm going to say, but to make it plain up front that what works for one drummer may be anathema to another. In other words, this advice is not etched in stone. I don't need to hear, "Spiggy Dunthumpin from jazthrashiphoppoworldmusic band The Dog's Breakfast tunes his drums completely opposite to yours, and his drums sound great." Good, say I, I'll catch his next gig and learn something more. The tuning advice that follows is what works for me as a starting point. The more I learn, the more I realise how little I know, and I'm constantly attempting to add to that knowledge by listening to, reading about and talking to good players of all styles.

You've probably already realised that the biggest single event that adds to your understanding of your set is the instance of actually playing it (assuming you're not playing in the same place every night, though even that...), so it logically follows that there isn't really any substitute for experience, although hopefully the following may shed a little light. Before going into the drums themselves, I'll look at several factors that I believe affect their sound and try to clarify what has become such a complex issue for many players.

## DRUM HEADS

There are now literally dozens of heads to choose from for each size of drum. No one can be expected to try every head available, but it helps to have a basic understanding of how the most popular models affect a drum.

We know that double-ply heads thicken the sound and cut down some overtones, but it's useful to find out about the variations available. Ask at your local drum shop; ask players who are using the heads you think may sound good on your drums; find out about alternative makes of similar models; enquire about the heads you think aren't suitable for you.

If you aren't keen on double-ply heads,

○ **Remo heads**

maybe you want heads with nothing between the plies or with additional damping. Some makes are more consistent than others. Get two heads — same size, make and model — hold one up and tap it lightly in the middle. Does it sound 'glassy'? Does the other one sound 'fatter', with more of a note to it? Make sure your top tom heads match up. If you like this head type on your bass drum, think how these inconsistencies may affect your sound.

If you prefer single-ply heads, ask about the different weights. Whether single or double-ply, an uncoated head will have a slightly more 'open' sound than a coated one. A thinner head on the bottom of a tom brightens its response, but I find it tends to cut the sustain somewhat. Bigger toms seem to require a different approach. I use heads of a heavier gauge underneath the larger

toms, and lighter ones on the bottom of the rack toms; this evens things out for me. Bear this in mind: a thicker head does not automatically equate with a bigger drum sound any more than a thin head does with a 'ringy' sound. Heads, like drums, resonate at an optimum point, and beneath or above that point the overtones are complex. This is not to say that drums have to be tensioned to that optimum point; just be aware and listen when you're tuning.

## SHELL TYPES

The same head configuration and tuning will not sound the same on different drums. Obvious I know, but thinner shelled drums with glue rings reinforcing the shell top and bottom have a different inherent sound from certain many-plied, dense shell types. (For example, I'd include DW and older

Ludwig and Slingerland in the former, and certain models by Sonor and Brady in the latter.) All of these well-made drums are capable of producing a wide range of sounds, but by their very nature will affect that hypothetical 'same head and tuning' scenario. Find out about the main characteristics of birch and maple, two very popular drum shell woods.

## SNARE DRUMS

It is not impossible, but you will have to work as hard to get a fat, thick sound out of a 13"x3" brass shell as you will a cutting crack from a 14"x7" wood shell. When we play live, even if we can afford several snare drums, we can only play one or two at a time. Don't try to fight the inherent sound of your (main) snare. If you have a 14"x5.5" wood or metal snare, you are right in the middle and, in my view, can go either way to some degree. Fatter? Double-ply head/medium tension/slightly looser snares. More crack? Single-ply/higher tension/snares slightly tighter. Pertinent to both examples: bottom snare head tight (try it a little looser for the 'fat' sound). Don't over-tighten the snares themselves — it chokes the drum. If you must damp, try one of these methods:

**1.** *A thin 'O' ring*

**2.** *A quarter of an 'O' ring held in place with a piece of tape to the rim, placed either nearest to you or furthest away.*

**3.** *Two or three pieces of masking tape (on top of each other) approximately three to four inches by three-quarters of an inch, placed between the five and seven o'clock positions on your batter head.*

**4.** *A small piece of masking tape (or gaffer tape) rolled back on itself at the twelve o'clock position on the head. (Or, try two pieces at nine and three o'clock.)*

## HOW HARD YOU PLAY

Contrary to popular belief, I don't agree that to get the best sound out of a drum you have to hit it as hard as possible. The simple, substantial proof of the point is that there are too many players out there getting great sounds without beating seven bells out of their kits. There is nothing wrong with playing hard, but there is nothing wrong with not playing hard either. Something that definitely doesn't help your sound no matter how heavy or light you play, is not hitting properly. Try not to dig into the drum; don't leave the stick on the head. Attempt to lift the sound from the drum by snapping the stick back. Snap your fingers, and then apply that sensibility to playing the drum. If you do play hard, you're probably better off with those double-ply heads because of the durability factor, but try the tension a little tighter than you would normally. The pitch that seems right when you sit behind the kit could be a dull thud by the time the sound has travelled a few feet and the rest of the band gets going. Perceived pitch drops as you move away from it.

The other factor under this header is where you are hitting the drum. It's accepted that the whole of the drum can and should be played, but if you're attempting to be consistent with your sound, be consistent with where on the head you strike. Of course, go off-centre for different sounds, but strive to keep those stick marks in as small a radius as possible. And this doesn't just apply to rock players pounding out a backbeat, by the way; check out the heads on any good jazz player's set.

## THE ROOM YOU ARE PLAYING IN

Small, 'dead', carpeted recording studio booth. Large, 'live' recording studio. Local pub. British Legion Club. Albert Hall. Wembley Arena. Open air to 50 people. Open air to a couple of hundred thousand people. I still haven't figured it out, but I'm always discovering new things.

In a small, 'dead' environment, I've found it pointless to attempt to power my way through. It's of little use adopting the "my kit sounded great in that 'live' club yesterday, so I'm going to hit it even harder" way of thinking.

You hit the floor tom. It goes ping with horrible overtones. My first reaction is to slacken it off very slightly. Try taking the bottom heads down by a specific amount (each tension rod by 45 degrees, for example); now try the same with the top heads. Not too sure? Take the bottom head back to where it was (the advantage of measured key tuning). Maybe a little more damping on the bass drum. Try not to be too extreme. Keep some of that ring/overtone in there or you'll sound like a cushion warehouse when the other players get going. Try the snare batter head up a little; maybe the four rods furthest away from you by a 90 degree turn each. Always remember that you have to project, and that while being a hard hitter helps, so does good tone and a clean execution and delivery.

The live sounding studio/stage/hall is very seductive, by which I mean that at its best, it seems to instantly make your drums sound great. But be careful...

**1.** *Do the toms match up and sound like they belong to the same set?*

**2.** *The drums sound great, but are the cymbals now overpowering the kit?*

**3.** *The snare: is the snare buzz from that second rack tom excessive?*
*Possible solutions: i. turn the snares off and play a medium hard single beat on each tom. (I'll go into tom tuning later); ii. in just about any given situation, part of the answer is to ease back on the cymbals. This can be made easier if your set is miked up; the sound man will ease the cymbals back in the mix.*

The following applies to a live room in a studio as much as it does to a live room in an un-miked performance-with-an-audience one. Substitute that 14″ extra thin you were using as a splash cymbal for one of your crashes and make one of the heavier crash cymbals the ride — play it nearer the bell to improve the definition. The reduction of the cymbals will balance the set; in the studio, the engineer will be able to use more of the ambient (room) mikes, which will give the drums their bigger sound without the cymbals drowning them out.

Whichever tom is causing the snares to rattle excessively will be the one which is closest in pitch to the snare with the snares off. Get them further apart from each other, tighten the snare and slacken the tom or vice-versa. On the snare (bottom) head, loosening the four tension rods surrounding the snares themselves is an often mentioned solution, but one I use as a last resort, as it invariably affects the relative tension of the snare wires and makes the drum start to sound choked.

## WHAT TYPE OF MUSIC/HOW MANY MUSICIANS?

I'm not going to attempt to list a million styles of music here; I'll confine myself to a few examples. If these seem obvious and common sense-ish, then so be it. Bear in mind they're there to make a point about tuning your set for the music and location. Two obvious extremes: a metal band with ancillary keyboard and brass players, and a lounge trio playing background music. Like I said, obvious. But start to think about all the obvious permutations. The trio adds a guitarist and some brass and plays a big hall... The metal band goes basic and does some warm-ups at a tiny club... If you care about how you sound, you'll want to change to fit those variations.

Sometimes my approach is that the more you have to project through, the more overtones you can get away with. However,

I've found that even that does not always apply (eg. hearing Elvin Jones at Ronnie Scott's, or Steve Gadd with Paul Simon at Wembley). Conclusion: there are no rules. One thing I've found consistently helpful over the years, though, is to hear my own drums away from them. In a studio, no problem. On a concert tour, I always get the best would-be drummer (musician/technician) I can find to play a simple beat while I listen out front. Be careful though; he/she plays harder or lighter, off-centre, 'digs in' more or less... Take that into account. Is the amount of ring/sustain/overtone similar on all the toms? How much will get absorbed by other instruments? In a lot of situations (that British Legion Club, for example) this is not always possible, but next time one of those arises, stand facing your set, back to the audience, and hit a rack tom. I bet it sounds different from when you hit it sitting at your stool.

## MICROPHONES

I think the 'no rules apply' maxim is probably more pertinent to this section than any other. I've had great results when all the factors were against me (less than ideal drum room, mike selection, time available etc.), and sometimes less than ideal results in a great room with lots of expensive mikes. Here are some random jottings...

If the engineer tells you that some of your toms are ringing excessively and they want to get them (a gate is a device that essentially closes down a mike after it has received a signal), politely request that he/she waits until they hear the kit in context with the rest of the musicians. Ask to hear a playback (in a live situation, get someone to play the offending drums), and if it still sounds bad, own up and do something about it! Remember, it's in the engineer's interest as much as yours for you to sound as good as possible.

If you've made your alterations and things still aren't ideal, offer these suggestions. If the snare sounds a little choked, try backing the snare mike off an inch or two. Alter the position of the bass drum mike before you again change your damping or tuning. If you prefer to play with a tighter batter head on the bass drum, you may have to damp it a little more than you would choose, though this does depend on your musical environment. For a little more bottom end on a tom, try moving the mike a little closer toward the middle of the drum and/or closer.

A word about the snare/hi-hat relationship. Those 15″ heavy hi-hats with the flanged edges that you've borrowed for your first recording session and which sounded great in your friendly music shop... forget 'em. The engineer will hate them because they'll leak down the snare mike more than the snare drum itself. That's something else to bear in mind next time you decide to upgrade.

No matter what your stylistic musical preference is, or whether you're in a million pound recording studio or the Bucket And Ferret pub with two mikes on the kit, work with the engineer. Often the smallest of adjustments will achieve the right result. For example, if you're adamant about not removing your front bass drum head and the sound isn't quite making it, try that head a mite slacker with a little damping on it. Remember that the mike — and consequently what's at the end of the audio chain — will hear things differently from you sitting between two and four feet away.

## THE DRUMS THEMSELVES

I don't know how many of you start off with a new snare drum or kit in a rehearsal room or on tour, but most of the time when I've got a new piece of equipment, the first place I can spend time with it is at home. If this is the case with you, don't tune it up and then take it to your next rehearsal/gig, tune it up and give it a few hits in different rooms. You

✪ **The snare drum: the most used piece of the kit**

may be surprised at how much the sound seems to change. (I personally avoid the kitchen: all my drums sound great in the kitchen!) You may then want to tweak them a bit to achieve a better 'mean' or 'average' sound before trying it in situ.

## THE SNARE DRUM

How much time have you got? Because most of us play this drum more than any other, and because now, more than ever, they come in a bewildering range of materials and sizes, this really is a 'how long is a piece of string' scenario. This is how I start...

First, the bottom head. Snares removed, get the tension rods finger-tight, and then, with a cloth or yellow duster lying in the middle of the head, depress it gently and look for the wrinkles around the edge. This should tell you whether the head is on evenly. Snare wires that go beyond the edges of the drum usually mean there's no snare bed cut into the shell; snares shorter than the head diameter mean there probably is. If there's no snare bed, pull the head down evenly. Avoid turning the key more than 360 degrees at any one time while you're checking with the cloth or duster that the wrinkles are disappearing evenly. If you're still getting wrinkles near one tension rod, tighten that one gradually until they disappear. Next, slacken all the tension rods by an equal amount, say two or three turns, and then start to slowly tighten the head again still using that cloth to press gently in the centre. If the drum does have a bed cut into it, tighten the four rods around the snare wires by two or more turns (each rod) after the first pass on the whole head. On most snare drums, I recommend you tune this head fairly tight. Only when using deeper shelled models, when I'm after a thicker sound, do I use a medium tension on the bottom head.

A word about the snares themselves: a duff set can ruin an expensive, well tuned drum. Turn the drum upside down with the snares on. Now, slowly release the snare mechanism. If the snares lose their shape, become disfigured and pull off to one side (one side gets tighter, the other looser), they've either been mistreated or not put on the drum correctly. The worst thing you can do to a set of snares is pull your finger across them when they've been tensioned. Make sure they tighten evenly as you pull the mechanism on, and also make sure they're clean; a lot of crap comes up from the bass drum pedal and the floor after a few weeks of heavy playing.

Now to the batter head. I tend to tension this in much the same way (finger-tighten the rods etc.). The main difference here is that I put the drum on the floor and kneel on the middle of the head. I don't recommend this if you've ever been mistaken for Luciano Pavarotti. However, it does make the wrinkles easier to detect, particularly if you're using a double-ply head. It also has the advantage of 'stretching in' the head. After I've eliminated the wrinkles, I slacken the rods by three or four turns, turn the drum around by approximately a third, and start to tension again. I often find that when I think I've got the head even, wrinkles appear after I've

tuned the drum. I probably do this (tighten/slacken/move the drum) about three or four times. What this should give you is the head on the shell about as evenly as it gets. Now things get very personal...

What I do is this. Assuming twelve o'clock is the rod furthest away from you and six o'clock the nearest, twelve gets two extra turns, eleven and one get one and a half turns, and ten and two get one. Seven and five get slackened by one turn, and six by two. All approximate because, as we know, snare drums don't have twelve tension rods, but you get the general idea. This has two effects: it cuts down some of the overtones, and gives more depth when you play rimshots, which, means my back beat. It's not so apparent with the heavier, cast-type hoops, but it's noticeable with the more common triple-flange style. That's my method, and whether or not you decide to give it a try, here are three final suggestions:

**i.** *If you prefer a medium tension, tune the batter head just that bit tighter than you think you should.*

**ii.** *If you have to damp the drum, use less than you think you should.*

**iii.** *Try the snare tension a little looser than usual. What you'll lose in pin-point definition you'll gain in perceived size of sound.*

A word about 'O' rings. They come in many widths and thicknesses and consequently all change the sound by varying amounts. As well as damping the drum, they also lower its perceived pitch. Try cutting one in half (or quarters) and using it. Beware of regarding 'O' rings as bearers of instant 'perfect snare sound'; apply judiciously.

## TOMS
The basic tuning method is the same as that

for the batter head on the snare, but be careful if you're using thin 'resonant' heads on the bottom. As you know, drums do have an optimum point where they ring and resonate more than at any other. This is not difficult to find if the heads are on evenly.

'Even tension or bottom head tighter or vice versa?' I hear you ask. Well, you'll really have to experiment to find out what works best for you, but knowing the head is on the drum evenly has to improve your odds. (We're assuming here, as with all drums, that the bearing edges are straight — in other words, that the head is sitting on a completely even surface.) If you're using a thinner head on the bottom, you can try it a little tighter. There is a line of thinking applicable to this combination that goes: 'bottom head for pitch, top head for tone'. In other words, the liveness or deadness comes from the tension of the top head, while the bottom head determines how high or low the note is.

Another popular method is to sit the tom on the floor, tap the head lightly in the middle, and 'remember' (or tape record) the note. Then turn the drum upside down and attempt to get the other head the same. This works best if you're using the same head configuration. If you're after a shorter, more fusionesque type of sound, you need to tune your drums above the ideal or sweet spot. If you want that 'hanging in mid-air' sound that suits gaps between beats, you need to tune to that sweet spot. Most of us are after the best of both worlds, and that can only be achieved by finding out what the drum is capable of doing.

Tom sizes: some more subjective observations...

**i.** *I'm less than convinced about the merits of 'power' sizes. In my opinion they're harder to tune, haven't got as much sustain as conventional sizes, and tend to boom.*

**ii.** *If you're using a three tom set up, it's going to be harder to get a discernible interval between them, and retain a similar tone, if the sizes are (hypothetically) 12"x8", 13"x9" and 14"x14". If you're using a 12/13/14 combination as part of a bigger setup, say with an 8" and a 10" above, and 16" below, fine, but you get my drift. Putting my money where my mouth is, I've recently ordered a kit with these three tom sizes: 10"x8", 13"x9" and 16"x14".*

If your set is the type where the tom holder goes into the shell, listen to how the drum sounds with the rod or tube all the way in, and then retracted as far as possible. You may wish to move the holders around to maximise what sounds best.

If you feel your floor tom (on legs) hasn't as much sustain or ring as your rack toms, try a small piece of dense rubber foam or a small square of carpet underneath each of the legs. Also, try the floor tom angled towards you, the bottom head not parallel to the floor. Conversely, if the tom has too much ring but you're happy with the tuning, try temporarily removing the rubber feet. You may find that your floor tom has an unpleasant (no sustain) type of ring that you wish to get rid of. This could be the 'beachball' or 'basketball in the gym' effect. This is sometimes caused by an over-reflective or glossy surface on the inside of the shell, and it tends to be more noticeable with bigger toms. The effect can be lessened by placing strips of masking tape vertically down the shell in between the lug screws. It might not look too great, but it's unlikely to have an adverse effect upon the audience's appreciation of your twenty minute solo.

Another observation: I've noticed a tendency recently for the smaller drums on multi-tom sets to be tuned proportionally a lot higher than the middle range toms, while the batter head on the largest drum seems almost to be flapping. I feel that the smaller

✪ Toms: bottom head for pitch, top head for tone

drums of the set should have the same tonal characteristics as the medium range, but at a higher pitch. The larger toms should match up too, and not sound like small bass drums from another kit. If you do want a different sound in the higher register, try different heads or some small Rototoms.

I have to add that the RIMS tom suspension system is a great idea and definitely helps the sound — highly recommended.

## BASS DRUM

Let me begin this final section by exorcising a personal gripe. I fail to see the point in purchasing a large bass drum (eg. 24″x20″) and inserting a three inch thick piece of foam all the way round the inside of the shell. If you want a big drum then use it. Right, now that's out of the way...

These days there seems to be a general movement towards the batter head being tuned slacker than the front, with the relative tensions being up to you to try out. But once again, make sure the head is on evenly. For most of my situations (not the jazz gig at my local) I have the batter head fairly slack and the least amount of damping I can get away with inside the shell (these days that usually means the Evans EQ pad). If damping is required, try out a small pillow or cushion, shredded newspaper or a blanket. Different positions (eg. just touching the batter head) will all affect the sound.

In the recording studio, just about anything goes — different head tensions/more damping/no damping/front head on/front head off... whatever works for the music. For 'live' work (miked up), I try to have as small a hole as possible in the front head (5″ in a 22″) so that the head still makes some contribution to the overall sound. A big (say, 12″) hole in a 22″ will leave a front head which does no more than keep the damping in place. In any case, if you do decide on a hole in the front head, I

recommend that the tension should be low.

If you not miked up, try the front head with a smaller hole, maybe with no damping, or even (gasp!) try a front head with no hole at all. Depending on your musical situation, you may have to damp that front head a little (using a felt strip near the edge, for example). Also, the drum will project better with a higher tension on the front head.

You've probably made up your mind by now about the beater type you're happiest with, but what about the impact point on the head? There are a fair few options: a click pad, a moleskin pad, a 50p coin, nothing at all. I used a click pad for a while but recently stopped because, although it helped the drum cut through in dense musical situations, I could still hear it in an unacceptable way above the drum. However, it may work perfectly well for you. I use a couple of pieces of plastic stuck together (similar in weight to a heavier 'O' ring), about 1.5″ square, held in place by two small pieces of gaffer tape. This puts sufficient definition on the front of the note without changing the sound of the drum. If you're unconvinced about some of these options, try them out by using tape to hold them in place before you glue them permanently onto the desired spot. By the way, for that occasional jazz gig I use an 18″ bass drum with both heads tuned medium tight.

## SOME THOUGHTS ON EQUIPMENT

When I first got interested in playing the drums (very many moons ago, my son), there were two or three good brands on the market while the rest were... let's say... interesting. This is most definitely not the case today. Although most manufacturers have a starter, middle and top set of drums in their range, the quality of all the so-called professional equipment available is of the highest order. This leads me to my final gripe. Anyone, and I mean anyone who tells

✪ **Heads on with care and tune your own sound**

## Practice Made Perfect

Practice — the scourge of the musically challenged and the fixation of the great. Whether you believe the argument of the scientist or the artist, there is no doubt that the only way to progress as a musician is through constant and repetitive practice. Like everything on the winding and uphill road to achievement, the raw stuff of diligent exercise manifests itself in the finished product of skill. The talent which shines so very brightly in many brilliant musicians is little more than a tiny pebble in the foundation of competent ability. Ask a successful drummer and they will tell you, "Man cannot become great on talent alone." So if your desire is to become the top cat of all styles, not just the master of some, you're going to have to knuckle down to some really hard graft.

Now, if you decide you want to get yourself physically fit, all you have to do is toddle off to any high street and be faced with the dilemma of which health club to visit. On the other hand, purely because we belong to a strange sect of people whose wont it is to bash lumps of wood across tensioned plastic and hammered metal, your choice of venue for physical expansion is indubitably restricted. Very few people have the luxury of being able to practice live drums at home, so finding a place to stretch your percussive touch is a vital start to any considerations of practice.

A crucial and prominent thought when considering practice has to be that any method of practice is better than none. Even the crudest form of work can be of help; just because you can't get to your kit doesn't mean you're excused from exercising. A practice kit could hold the answer. If you're worried about the expense, just go out and steal one — only joking. If you don't have the money to splash out on a complete practice kit, rig up a pad for the bass drum

you that A is great and B is rubbish is full of it. This applies to drums, cymbals, heads and just about everything else. I'm tired of hearing about one brand being hopeless, and such and such a player said so, and now he/she uses Brand X and says they're great. Twaddle! Make up your own mind. We've all been influenced by what our favourite players use — I'm no exception — but make your buying decision based on what your ears tell you, not on the advertisements. Add your experience to the 'who's playing what' factor. That snare drum you're thinking about getting — would you be interested if it didn't have that brand name on it? Of course, a quality brand name is an indication of an instrument well made — my point is to get you to consider the alternatives. Cards on the table and kudos where it's due time: I use and endorse Yamaha drums, Zildjian cymbals, Evans heads, RIMS and Pro-Mark sticks, but I use them because in my opinion they have a slight edge and they suit me. One of my favourite players — for his great sound as well as his playing — uses a DW/Paiste/Remo combination. In conclusion, put your drum heads on carefully, keep experimenting, and make your own sound. Good luck!

✪ **The higher the quality of practice input, the less time you need to dedicate to it**

and one for the snare, attach your pedal and you're away. On just these two surfaces you can master many areas of your playing, and it's especially useful when combined with time on your real kit, allowing you to really go to town on your playing weaknesses. If at times you're forced to practice without pads at all, it's possible to work through certain co-ordination exercises by sitting in a drumming position, taking up your sticks and cultivating new objectives. All you have to do is tap your feet on the floor and your sticks on your knees (or a cushion if you're a hard hitter). This type of exercise will enhance your aptitude for tricky problems and make your mind more open to solving the usual obstacles that tend to trip us all up. The muscles in your limbs will benefit, and it will give you an impressive head start when you return to your kit.

I've also experimented with a method for stretching the muscles in the feet, legs and ankles. Sit on a high surface and hook your toes through the handle of a small bucket or paint pot filled with stones or weights. Then slowly lift your toes by pivoting your ankles up and down. This action will slowly develop the muscles in your toes and shins. I found this a useful exercise for developing my left foot.

None of these aids are in any way a total substitute for real practice, but when you are unable to use your real kit, they will be of benefit.

Once you've organised suitable facilities, it's important to design a regime that will fully utilise the time you have available to work. When I first started to play seriously, I was hounded by tales of other drummers managing 23 hours practice, seven days a week. It is crucial to remember that a lot of these stories aren't true, and anyway, it's better to work at a pace with which you are not only happy, but which is also convenient and feasible for you to execute. It's silly to try and emulate what you have heard others claiming. 'Little and often' is a good motto.

If you do something for half an hour to an hour every day, with total dedication, within six months you'll be proficient and within a year you'll be an expert.

The next subject to consider is maintaining a high quality of practice input. It's a sure fire fact that the higher the quality of your practice, the less time you need to dedicate to it, and the more you will achieve in the time spent. If you're capable of maintaining high concentration levels and constantly work in elements at which you are not proficient, the fruits of your training will be richer and will steal less much less of your time. Your attention should be focused at all times on the problem you're attempting to solve. It's good to set time goals for each specific exercise or objective; for example, learning a certain style for twenty minutes and sticking with it strictly for this time. Long term objectives clearly laid out in writing are the first step towards realising your playing aspirations. When you find your attention wandering, look to these guidelines to put your mind back on course. If you can map out gentle steps of progression to endlessly push you forward, it's much easier to see where you're heading; and each small step of attainment helps you to see that long term projects are possible, and that all this hard work is very worthwhile.

Having taken all this into account, a problem which still faces you is that all musicians must bless themselves with an abundance of saint-like patience. Technique and skill development can seem painfully slow, and, even worse, once you believe you have accomplished a certain skill, your aptitude to perform it suddenly disappears. Sometimes, when you sit behind your kit, it feels like your playing is awkward, amateurish and cumbersome; it almost feels like your hands are tired and you're never going to play well again. When this happens, take faith in the fact that your skill will return, sometimes even better than before.

I'm told it's quite normal, but it doesn't half piss me off. It's best to just keep slowly chipping away at the problem. Don't despair, it's not just drummers; most musicians are forced to wait long periods before new ideas can even be contemplated in a live situation.

There is a method I've used with good results, a technique to speed up the process of goal attainment. It's a principle of cramming practice by exercising a specific style or objective for a prolonged period over two or three days. Set aside one hour to occupy yourself purely with just one topic, monotonously repeating the project at a slow speed and gradually building up in tempo until your proficiency at this skill is clearly etched on your brain. If continued for two or three days, it becomes a perfect foundation to perform whatever skill it is, and a rapid way to break in new and difficult tasks. It's imperative that you don't stop playing for the entire hour, filling every minute with relevant input. It is okay to change exercises round to make the time more interesting, and use the metronome to build up the tempo, but don't stop. This is, of course, not a method of progressing from novice to expert, but if you're tackling individual broken-down sections, it will work.

Having convinced you to practice non-stop for an hour, I'm now going to totally contradict myself and stress how important it is to take short breaks from your endeavours. It's only really important though to take quick rest periods if you're pushing a certain muscle to play harder and faster; giving it a minute's rest will improve the quality of the exercise, allow for some blood to flow around the muscle and prepare it for the next onslaught of rapid hammering. This increases your stamina and allows your practice session to be extended. If at any time your limbs start to hurt excessively, it's best just to stop there and then. If it's just a slight fatigue pain, try to

stand it for about ten to fifteen seconds. Within your total practice time, regular short breaks will help to evade the boredom-based monotony that often entices you to throw in the towel. It is important to know when you've come to the end of useful practice time — it's the point when you reach the equilibrious stage of tiredness and mental burnout. When this happens, go to the pub, there is no point in going on.

The other side of the personal furtherance coin is developing your ability to utilise your mental agility to augment your artistic talents and make them shine out. The two main constituents of this skill are memory and concentration. Attempting to stretch your memory is a hard problem, and as far as I know, there are few methods for successful development. If you're in a situation where there is little rehearsal time, your mind has to be clear and extra-perceptive to each song, each tempo, and every change. A problem I find when trying to remember something is that, at the time I'm so confident that I've recorded all the information correctly in my head, but later this confidence reveals itself to be false, and I have great difficulty in recalling anything. My solution is to make many notes and mentally label all the important parts of the music. Mental contemplation of your band's live set and all the bits you play, working through each song in your head, is a very useful preparation. It is also good for you to play the top line melody with a pair of sticks on a practice pad. Obviously you can't play all the notes, but go through each song accenting the singing parts and solos, either on a walkman or from memory. This really helps with placing the parts correctly.

Concentration is the second and most important mental discipline. Prolonged concentration is what I consider to be the thing that splits the average musician from the true master. As with memory power, it is difficult to quantify how to improve your concentration; but before I play, I clear my

✪ **Concentration is the second and most important mental discipline**

mind of all though, relax and breathe deeply. I then focus sharply on the task ahead, seeing clearly in my mind everything I'm about to perform. When I'm practising, I experiment with how long I can keep a solid groove going on the kit, without any deviation onto the toms or cymbals. After just a few minutes, will power and concentration are thrown squarely into the spotlight for severe scrutiny. One tiny glitch in your concentration and your hands are aching for just a little pat on the toms. After about fifteen minutes, it feels like your kit is surrounded by a circle of used car salesmen, all loudly persuading you that it would be okay for just one quick run round the kit.

So put your mind to it; it is, after all, your brain that tells your limbs what to do, so the basics of every task are laid deep within your head. Being in charge of your brain enhances everything you play.

I hope you can extract at least a small amount of use from these pages. It's good to remember that not everyone's perception of problems, cures and education is the same; something that one person has difficulty with, another will perform with natural ease. Hopefully there are crossover points where ideas can meet and be of use to us all. Never forget, you don't ever stop learning, it's good to get as many teachers, tutor books and videos as you can, and squeeze them dry for new information. In order to improve, you must think of your mind as a huge sponge, eager to soak up new and challenging concepts, theories and practices.

Practice should also be carried out totally voluntarily, your desire to achieve pushing you forward rather than a guilty feeling that you haven't done enough. Some parents and teachers tend to motivate rehearsal and practice in the wrong way. It must always be fun and not a chore, otherwise it's not worth doing.

So if you want to crack the knack and have the badge of drumming authority

shining brightly on your chest, set your mind to serious, worthwhile, quality practice. It may not be easy, but it can be fun.

The only item you really need to remember is that all your efforts must be ever onward and upward. Each time you practice, the exercise should either be harder to achieve or a brand new skill. If you listen to someone practising and they're playing with considerable finesse, the chances are they are only recovering ground that they've already traversed; whereas if you hear someone struggling or messing up parts as they practice, they will probably be half way towards perfecting a new technique and expanding their abilities. So there you have it in a nutshell: if you want to sound good, sound crap.

## Sweeping Statements

Some drummers treat them with suspicion; some laugh at them; many don't understand them at all; and yet some depend on them to earn a living. Okay, so what am I talking about? Cars? Managers? Drugs? Well, I'm actually referring to, as Weckl puts it, the 'lost art' in drumming today — the brushes.

Brushes are often overlooked by today's players, and any number of reasons could apply. Some think that the brushes are inappropriate; others think they are out of date. Some drummers even think it wimpish to play with brushes. In many ways, this is a sad state of affairs, because in rejecting and ignoring the brushes, they are actually turning their backs on a whole world of expression and technique. Moreover, they could come severely unstuck in the event of finding themselves at a gig where brushes have to be used — not only in terms of ability either. I mean, where in the name of Erskine can you get brushes at nine o'clock on a Saturday night? The only brushes you'll come across in that situation will be given to you by your musical director — and they'll be with death.

So it's obviously a sound idea to keep at least one pair of brushes in your sticks bag — ready when required. But, of course, you don't need to be too clever to realise that it's no good going into your local music shop and saying, 'Could I have a pair of brushes, please?' That would be about as useful as going into Our Price and asking, 'Could I have a record, please?' There are — probably literally — hundreds of different types of brushes available, so it would make sense to have an idea of what's on offer before troubling the assistant (who's probably a keyboard player anyway) with your protestations.

Essentially, types of brushes can be divided into two broad categories — those with metal filaments, and those with plastic. The latter types are a relatively new development, whereas their metal counterparts have been around for decades. The manufacturers of plastic filamented brushes are quick to point out the so-called 'advantages' of their products; for example, no scratches on the cymbals, minimal head surface wear etc.. There is, however, one important fact which they don't tell you. Plastic brushes are noticeably quieter than metal ones. And what of the latter? Well, the filaments are springy, as opposed to the shock-absorbing characteristics of the former, which can be an advantage in many playing situations. They also give a brighter, more 'toppy' sound on the cymbals. However, they can tarnish quite quickly, and this dirt can easily transfer to drum heads and cymbals. In advanced cases, it'll tend to make the filaments stick together in clumps, removing some of the 'brushy' characteristics of the sound. Also, the filaments will bend rather than snap when over stressed — for example, when inadvertently caught between the head and

the hoop — and can be quite difficult, in not impossible, to bend back.

My personal favourite is an English brand called Zok. This is a light, plastic-filamented type of brush, easy to play with and cheap to replace. However, I always keep a pair of metal-filamented brushes to hand, ready in the event of playing some authentic jazz which calls for that definitive 'scrape' on the snare drum. You will probably find your local music shop, especially if it specialises in drums, has a fair selection and could advise on different makes. Prices start from around £4 or £5 and can rise to about fifteen or more for some highly specialised types.

Okay, so you've bought your brushes, pedalled home nineteen-to-the-dozen and sat yourself behind the kit. Now what? Well, take your duffel coat off first — it restricts your movement.

Probably the easiest way to get started is to use the brushes as you would use sticks — try doing a few fills and rhythms. The first difference you'll notice is in the volume — brushes are much quieter than sticks. Also, you'll probably find that you're fluffing a few ruffs and so on. The explanation is very simple: there's little bounce to cheat with. The sad truth of the matter is that every single note that you play has to be sticked (or should that be brushed?) properly — no buzz rolls here! Even so, without much practice, you'll probably find yourself feeling fairly comfortable and playing away quite merrily. Using the brushes as 'quiet sticks' is very common for drummers playing small venues or cocktail gigs, and you'll probably find it easier to hit the drums comfortably without incurring the wrath of the management. When using plastic brushes in this way, you may find it useful to gaffa the filaments together in a bundle about an inch and a half from the end to give a more precise feel. Although this is helpful, it does render the brushes useless for playing swing, when you need the 'spread' of the filaments. It also makes it impossible to push the filaments back into the handle. A word of warning here, though: don't try this with metal filaments — it's like playing with a couple of hosepipes.

After a while playing around like this, you'll probably begin to realise that using the brushes as stick substitutes has its advantages. If you can develop a good technique for this, you'll open up for yourself a new dimension in playing quietly — the riffs you want to play at the volume other people want to hear them. Even so, the use of brushes on the drum kit doesn't stop here. There's a wealth of further applications to be examined; and some of them are so different from using sticks that they will need a fair amount of practice before they can be mastered.

Probably the most common of these applications is the 'sweep'. As its name suggests, this involves pushing the brush across the drum in order to produce a scraping sound. It should be pointed out that if you are using plastic-filamented brushes, you should make sure that the ends of the filaments are in good condition. They can go a bit 'furry' in time, and this will drastically reduce the volume of the scraping sound. Also, of course, the sound will be much more pronounced if coated heads are used, rather than clear ones.

Try brushing with the left hand in a continuous sweep at the left hand side of the snare drum head while tapping out a swing pattern with the right hand (one, two and three, four and etc.) on the right hand side of the head. It also helps the rhythm along tremendously if the hi-hat is played (with the foot) on beats two and four. This may seem quite straightforward, but its execution on the snare drum is not as easy as you may think. It really does test your independence, trying to get the left hand to sweep and the right hand to tap at the

same time; but stick with it because it does offer an authentic, 'jazzy' brush sound.

Of course, this is not the only way of playing jazz with brushes. The great Ed Thigpen of the Ella Fitzgerald band, is a wonderful exponent of the finer points of brushwork, and employs a variety of techniques to gain his unique sound. Probably the modern-day champion of brushes on the drum kit is Dave Weckl, who not only uses them in their traditional setting, but also finds other applications for them, even in so-called 'pop' music. An interesting example of this can be found on Chick Corea's Elektric Band album *Eye Of The Beholder*, where on the track 'Home Universe', Weckl uses the brushes to great effect. Light, syncopated snare drum riffs combine with a steady hi-hat part to create an entirely unique feel, perfect for the track in question.

Of course, no article on brushwork would be complete without a mention of Philly Joe Jones. With his superlative playing alongside the likes of Charlie Parker, Miles Davis and Sonny Rollins, his name has become synonymous with the brushes. Any drummer interested in playing with brushes could do a lot worse than to study his work. In his book *Brush Artistry*, Jones explains in detail how he achieves his sound and offers exercises for the student to practise. A valuable addition to any drummer's library.

The most important thing to remember about using brushes on drums is that it's fun — and it's different. For an investment of possibly as little as a fiver, you can add a wealth of expression to your musical vocabulary, and develop a talent you may not have even known you possessed. So, sweep your prejudices into the dustpan of drumming, dust off your abilities and try out something new.

# chapter 9
## No More Heroes

How things have changed. Looking back over just the last ten years of drumming, you can't help but notice how things have changed — faces, names and styles. But the oddest thing is the way drumming has diversified into countless diffractions of itself, and that there seem to be no more heroes like there were in the old days. There just don't seem to be as many big names as there used to be; and I'll tell you why, too. It's because there are more big names, and as a consequence, fewer big names, because being a big name isn't as big as it was because there are more of them. Geddit? While Vinnie is a big name — no denying it — his name is so big you only need to say half of it and the saliva begins to flow. So is Weckl. So is Dennis. So is Trilok. So is Chad. Airto... The list is endless — you get the picture. Ten years ago it was Steve Gadd, Steve Gadd's mum — or is that mom — and that was about your lot. When Phil Collins — bless his heart, what a nice bloke — lost it a bit — but what a geezer, loves his mum, mind — was finally captured by Rhythm for an interview, the editorial breathlessly gushed about the extra sales that his Phil-ness would generate. Because those were the days when giants roamed the earth. Even short ones like Phil.

However there's more to this than just big names and how big they are. Our entire appreciation of matters rhythmic has been undergoing huge changes in the last few years. The whole scene has changed to such an extent that compared to ten years ago, it almost resembles a utopian vision of the future. Clinics have gone from odd one-offs in upstairs rooms in pubs to organised and endorsed tours or events on the scale of the regular world-wide Zildjian Days. As a consequence there's less chance of having an accidental pint with the star after the show, but then modern clinics are like a gig or something, and at a gig you don't expect to have a beer with the stars. It's almost as though drummers have become a whole market to be tapped, rather than just another bunch of train spotter types. Obviously though, the nerd/bore image is something drumming can't totally shake off — there's always a couple of us at the front looking at the kit, and when you hear someone at these gigs talk about great chops, they don't mean lamb or pork, but who would have it any other way? The selling of drumming to drummers has never gone at such a pace, and although there was something very special about upstairs rooms in pubs, watching a drummer in amongst the torn pool tables, it's not exactly a step backwards that we want to

○ **Vinnie 'Saliva'**

make, is it? These days you can settle down to any one of a hundred videos — in the old days you made do with Buddy Rich's book ("Play slowly at first; increase speed gradually. Keep strict rhythm") — as well as more excellent product than you can shake a drumstick at. Drummers have never had it so good; it's almost like someone's built the train spotters a shed at the end of the platform.

What is odder still about this is that the heroes of yesteryear — and I'm talking about Stewart Copeland, Mel Gaynor and their ilk — were successful players in big (essentially) pop bands, shifting units. These two spring to mind because they were great players in chart-topping bands, which made them even more heroic given everyone's natural distrust of success in a market-driven business like music. Look at the short shrift your Duran Duran types get — though it must be said, he only really did the videos and doesn't deserve such a hard time. Even Arnold Schwarzenegger has a stunt double — the last thing the studio wants is the star to trip up, after all. While it's always been true that you could be a big name without really selling all that many records — and in jazz this has pretty much been the rule — music nowadays has diversified to the point where our

attention and respect is demanded from all quarters. And although there are reasons to be uncheerful about shows such as *Top Of The Pops* and the grip it has on music marketing, the charts are pretty diverse. No, they are. Being an indie band is now actually a career option rather than a commercial predicament. In fact 'Indie' is almost a contradiction in terms itself. The dance scene has entirely stepped the corporate blockade that the record companies represent, and thrives, ever changing, ever expanding. Just because we're not necessarily included doesn't mean it's diversity shouldn't be celebrated; the dance scene doesn't moan, though that may be whatever it is they put in their tea, as it were. Most amazing is that there hasn't been a full-blooded return to the pre-punk 'muso' tendency of the early Seventies. You'll find that the standard of playing at all levels is quite incredible — you don't have to seek our great players, nor is their membership of a chart topping band reason to distrust their ability. Vinnie plays for Sting for Chrissakes and we all still love him.

So how has this come about? Certainly ten years ago the writing appeared to be on the wall for the brotherhood of rhythm, being a drummer at the time wasn't unlike being a member of a dying breed. Fortunately all the dire predictions that were going around during the drum machine-infested mid-Eighties about the drummer going down on the Titanic (not a rude joke, thank you — though there must be a drummer somewhere with a mouth big enough) have not come true. What has happened is that after an initial struggle drummers have got their shit together to such an extent that drumming is leaping to new heights. You can find this everywhere; the techniques sections in drum magazines is proof of the level that their readers operate at — in theory of course; for all I know you're all sat on the bog, *Rhythm* in one hand, the beautiful gleaming chrome of the latest kit dazzling your eyes, and in the other hand...

# chapter 10
## The Gig Guide

### The Right Stuff

If you play the drums and are serious about making it your career, you'll certainly be aware of many top session players. But do you ever wonder how they achieved such a prestigious position? To reach the lofty heights of the elite few, you first have to join the army of session players who, while making a living from their drumming, still have to hunt down their next job. As one of those drummers myself, I hope to give you a few pointers on starting out in the jungle of pro session work. First of all, before you attempt to do anything, you must make sure that both you and your playing are up to it. You can't enter this world half-heartedly; it will take a long time, a great deal of hard work, and your total commitment.

### DO YOU PRACTISE EVERY DAY?
You must exercise your hands and feet regularly; get into the habit of a daily workout on your drums. You can only get out of your playing what you are prepared to put in.

### ARE YOU SUPPLE AND FIT?
Studios are often hired by the day, so breaks

✪ **Put down tracks that represent you well on good quality tape**

are rare and days can be long. Being on tour is also very tiring. Often, stamina can be one of your greatest assets.

### ARE YOU VERSATILE?
This doesn't mean being able to emulate a few Dave Weckl licks. It means being able to cover many styles, speeds, and having good natural timing. You also need to feel at home with a click track, both live and in the studio.

✪ **London, the scene of some of the most prestigious work**

### DO YOU HAVE GOOD, RELIABLE EQUIPMENT?

Your choice of gear is up to you, but it must be of reliable quality, and should be well tuned and in good working order at all times. You should always carry a spare snare drum, a set of replacement heads and plenty of sticks.

### CAN YOU READ MUSIC?

If you are considering session work, the answer undoubtedly has to be yes. But how long is it since you exercised this skill? Brush up on your reading, make sure it's instant and precise. You may not need it all the time, but without it you're throwing away potential work.

### ARE YOU NEAR POTENTIAL WORK?

Most session work will be in and around larger cities, the most prestigious being in London. Long journeys will make your days longer and more tiring.

### HAVE YOU RELIABLE TRANSPORT?

You must be able to transport both yourself and your kit anywhere, at any time. As a

session player, this will be your responsibility.

### ARE YOU EASY TO CONTACT?

You must have a telephone number and address at which you can be contacted at all times. It doesn't necessarily have to be your own, just somewhere reliable that will pass on all your messages. An answering service or machine is a good idea too.

If you're feeling confident about your answers to the above questions, you're now ready to start looking for work. Never be surprised at the lack of people queuing up to hire you — nobody knows you're here yet. Think of yourself as a company with a viable product to sell: you have to advertise yourself in the right places, to the right people. To get started, put together a package about yourself, containing a photograph, a biography and a recent recording of your playing. The easiest and cheapest way of doing this is to get a flattering black and white photo of yourself, photocopy it onto A4 paper, and add a brief history of your musical experiences, your influences, styles in which you excel, and any other information that might be useful.

✪ **Be contactable**

✪ **If you have no experience in a studio, offer to help out in one while they are recording drums**

You must make it as brief as possible. Don't forget to include your name, age and a contact number and address. If you've been featured in any press articles, copy and include them. On a good quality tape, put together a compilation of tracks that represent you well. Don't include tracks with programmed drums unless you are looking for work as a programmer. Finally, have some business cards made up — try to be as inventive as possible here, so people remember who you are.

Now to point your mind towards looking for work...

Unfortunately there is no magic formula that will immediately project you into the upper echelons of the session scene. It's a long, hard slog, and one that perfectly defines the snowball effect. You start with small local gigs or sessions, and as you build up your experience and contacts, so the work grows, providing you are constantly pushing to develop your career. The No. 1 rule is to accept every opportunity that comes your way; every time you play is an advert for your talents. Even things you have to do for little or no money may eventually lead to financially worthwhile engagements. Okay, it's easy for me to sit here and tell you to accept every opportunity that presents itself when, perhaps, you are not being offered any. If this is the case, head for your local library every week and check the current music press — don't forget a publication called *The Stage*. Hunt through the 'drummers wanted' section, take down all the details, phone the all up, and sort out the good from the bad. The first question I used to ask was, is there any money? Although the money isn't important at this stage, you can tell how serious they are from their reaction. Attend auditions and try for everything you think is worthwhile. Don't get disheartened by this process; it can be laborious and soul destroying, and you must expect a lot of rejections. But if you keep it up, it will pay off eventually.

Another way of searching for work is to send your biog to people who might be in the market for a drummer. Obviously this is a bit more hit and miss, but it can be very worthwhile. The most likely people to be looking for a drummer are local studios, bands without full-time drummers, record producers, and management companies. It's

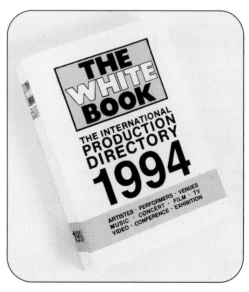

✪ **Virtually all companies in the music industry**

up to you to use your imagination and be inventive in finding ways of meeting these people and getting your biog to them. There are no rules and no game plan here; if you're serious about your playing, you will find a way to do it. One bit of advice, though: get hold of a copy of *The White Book*. It contains the name, address and phone number of virtually every company involved in the UK music industry. Needless to say, it's very useful.

Recording studios are a very important source of work for a session player. And to help you tap into this, here's a few ideas to get your foot in the door.

First you should contact all your local recording studios with the facility to record live drums. Visit them; let them know you are a session drummer, and that you're available for work. Give them a biog and a tape, tell them that you'll do the first session for free, and offer them a percentage of the fee for any sessions they arrange for you thereafter. Another option is to offer yourself free of charge, to help out on any personal projects they may have.

If you are not experienced in a studio situation, find a local studio and offer to help them out while they are recording drums. Get the engineer to teach you how to mike up a kit, and off to help for free. This is a great way to watch other drummers record, and you'll be in a good position to get cheap studio time, or even the odd session that might come up. Again, these are purely ideas; use your imagination to expand on them, and don't be afraid to learn, whatever standard of player you are.

You might also consider using an agency to help you find work, such as the Session Connection in London. Agencies can be a great source of work, but it's hard to get accepted by an established company unless you are established yourself. There's no harm in sending them a biog, but if you're just starting out, you'll probably have better luck looking for work on your own.

As you begin to be called for sessions, you'll realise how important it is to make the most of each client. You have to maximise the chances of them calling you back. Never consider a job to be unimportant just because it's low paying; next time they call you, they might have secured a huge deal and be prepared to pay whatever you want.

If you are given a tape to learn, play along with it and learn it inside out. If you're playing a track written by your client, they will be impressed if you know what you're doing. Don't just listen to it in your car on the way to the session.

Always turn up on time. This is one of the most important factors in a professional attitude. For studio sessions, it's important to get all your drums in and set up as quickly as possible — studio time is very expensive. Make sure you have the right gear for the session; check with the producer beforehand to find out exactly what you'll need — I've done a lot of studio work where I've only used a bass, snare and cymbals. I also have a selection of snare drums to give the producer as many options as possible.

When recording, always play your part as simply as possible. It's much easier for the producer to suggest you play a little busier than it is for him to complain that you are over-playing. If your part is as simple as the track allows, you'll be much more accurate and efficient. If you work fast, are well on time, and play what's required, I guarantee you'll be asked back. So always play what's asked of you, even if it feels awkward. As a session player you're being paid to play what they want to hear.

Be sure to treat everyone involved in the session with respect. Try to get on with everyone. This can often be difficult, but it's worth the effort; you'd be amazed how many times I've heard: "I had this guy in the other day. He turned up late, moaned about his fee, argued with the engineer... Good player, but I'll never use him again." Get yourself a good reputation early on.

So, to my final point. Once you have started to expand your contacts, it's essential to keep in constant touch with them. Call them up all the time and remind them that you're available for work — this is where most of your gigs will come from. Never stop hunting, try to be out playing every day of the week. Take an hour every day to think about and send off your biog to as many people as possible. I've been working as a session drummer for a few years now, and I still do all these things in order to keep working. Obviously the more people you know, the easier things get, but don't forget, you've got to get out and make those contacts in the first place.

These ideas should be of some help in getting your session career started. Remember, be prepared for every eventuality; offers of work will often spring up from nowhere, so make sure you're ready when they do. Keep up your practice, it's vitally important. And join the Musicians' Union, they can be very useful, especially if you're out there on your own. Keep your eyes open for every opportunity, and, to see you through those inevitable periods of unemployment, find a rich girl/boyfriend. That's it. Good luck, and —hey! — hold on to your dream.

# Stage Tight

### 1. CONFIDENCE TRICKS

Perhaps the most important aspect of any performance is confidence. If you're happy about what you're doing, it's easy to forget any nerves you may have beforehand, and start to really enjoy playing in front of an audience. This usually establishes a two-way channel of communication, because the punters can see that you're enjoying the gig, and it helps them to do the same (always assuming you're reasonably competent). This means that, at some

stage, you must have worked hard to learn the material and master any physical difficulties that may arise in its performance. Taking this as read, it is vitally important that: i. you know what you're doing, and ii. you are happy about doing it. Yes, I know it's obvious, but consider for a moment — you're the cornerstone that holds the whole band together, the foundation of the rhythmic base, providing a structure that can be built around. The band has to rely on you to be both constant and consistent — rock solid. If the rest of the band know that they can put their trust in your ability, it helps to build their confidence and allows the band to function as a tight unit.

Before a gig, apart from coping with the effects of the Battle of the Somme apparently being re-fought in your stomach, and the rapidly increasing desire to get to the john at ever more frequent intervals, there are a number of things which will almost certainly undermine your confidence and thereby affect the way you play.

### ARRIVING LATE

Apart from being very unprofessional, this invariably starts you off on the wrong foot. Tempers aren't usually improved by the fact that, when time's running short, anything that can go wrong usually will go wrong. Bass drums seem reluctant to leave the security of their cases, and stands appear to take on an almost deck chair-like complexity.

If you do manage to get a sound check, you're usually in such a flap, that as long everything sounds near enough okay, you end up making the sort of compromises that prove woefully inadequate midway through the first song, resulting in the complete inability to hear anything other than yourself and the rather nasty rattle coming from the back of the bass speaker stack.

It doesn't look good to be fiddling around with last minute adjustments to your kit — the stage still littered with empty drum cases — while the first punters are drifting into the gig; it ruins any impact when the band actually takes the stage. And because of the stress caused by trying to get everything done at light speed, your confidence takes a battering before you've even begun. Give yourself enough time to cope with any last minute crises and unavoidable delays — they occur at practically every gig.

## MENTAL APPROACH

Having the correct mental approach is, to a large extent, dependent on being in possession of a brain. Thankfully, this can be quickly and easily checked with the aid of a Black & Decker and a mirror. Once the existence of a certain amount of grey matter is established, however, it is of course essential to remember to bring it with you to the gig — you'll almost certainly need it.

As far as attitude is concerned, I'm afraid it comes to simply being relaxed. But that's the key to it, really; as any psychologist will tell you, relaxation is the best way of handling anxiety, and there can be few more anxious situations than waiting to step onto a stage. It tenses you up and inhibits your playing, undermining the confidence of both you and the rest of the band.

Try and arrange it so that you've got a few minutes at least, before you go on stage, when you can just sit very quietly and collect yourself — concentrate on relaxing every muscle in your body, and if things have been rushed, just slow yourself down, so that you walk on stage in control. Don't worry about feeling a little nervous — it's good for you, it has a purpose, it gets the adrenaline flowing and heightens your awareness and responses, and by the time you're midway through the second number, it'll have dissipated anyway.

If you're naturally a pretty cool cat, don't become too casual in your approach — nobody likes a smartarse, and over-confidence can lead to sloppiness and mistakes. Try to put a little edge to your performance (thinking about imminent nuclear destruction can often be useful in this respect). Above all, stay in control.

## DISAGREEMENTS

Unfortunately, it is seldom the case that the band that plays together, stays together; and if it's not going to fall apart on the first bad gig, or even the bad first gig, you'll have to try to exercise a little patience with the rest of the band, and maybe see things from their points of view when circumstances demand it. Above all, get to know what they're up against. If you cannot agree on something, it's better to agree to disagree... agreeably (don't you agree?). Bottling up feelings or trying to salvage a line of communication after having lashed out at someone either verbally or physically, is never easy, especially during a gig. And it's seldom very successful trying to play with a band who are wondering what you'd look like separated from your nose.

Don't ever adopt the attitude that you don't need the rest of the band; if you've any intention of 'making it', the only way you'll do it is by stickin' together — thick and thin, and all that.

## EQUIPMENT

It goes without saying that faulty equipment should be repaired before the night of the gig (unless, of course, the fault has occurred during the gig). Set your kit up at home and attend to anything that even comes close to being a fault, and if it can't be repaired properly, replace it.

Nobody who is even half-way serious about being a drummer should ever go out on a gig without a spare snare drum head,

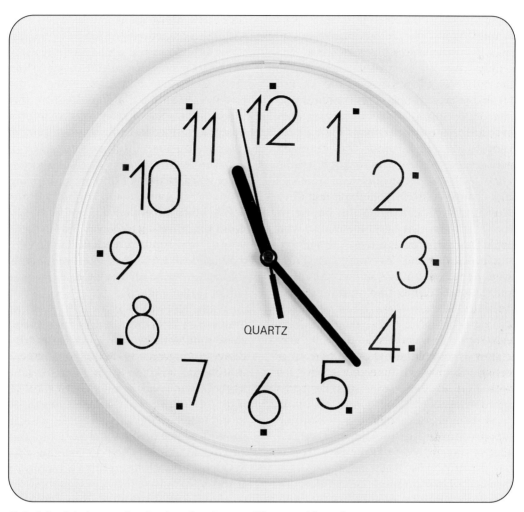

✪ Arriving late is unprofessional, undermines confidence and frays tempers

or preferably a spare snare drum. Okay, a very cheap one if necessary, but being able to instantly change what is arguably the most important drum of your outfit, has got to be worth thinking about. If you've got a roadie, make sure he has the spare instantly to hand so that it can be swapped over quickly; if you haven't, always keep the spare close to your kit during the gig.

Now, I know that for a lot of drummers, actually getting it together to buy a kit at all involves the sort of self-sacrifice worthy of a Trappist monk, and the prospect of shelling out on a duplicate drum which may never

be needed, can obviously be daunting. But just consider — after guitar strings, the snare drum skin is without doubt the most likely piece of hardware on the stage to go kaput (apart, perhaps, from the guitarist's brain), and it's also arguably one of the most important; so you owe it to yourself, the rest of the band, and the paying audience, to consider the proposition whenever the chance allows.

One way of getting more out of the idea is to actually use the second snare drum alongside the first (perhaps buy a piccolo, or tune it differently) to increase the sound capabilities of the kit. If a skin goes through, you've got the other there to take over — you need scarcely miss a beat.

Obviously other heads can, and do, go through, and other parts of the kit can break, but these problems are not nearly so difficult to play around as the snare, apart perhaps from the bass drum. However, it's hard to do much about this during a performance, unless you've got a roadie who can thread his way between your legs and change it while you're playing (I've seen it done), or wait till the interval if you're playing two sets. I suppose you could practise a real fast head change, pit-stop style, while the singer or guitarist tells them the one about the actress, the dwarf and the jar of Marmite; but however you do it, having a spare snare head ready and waiting is bound to help confidence-wise, as are spare tom-tom heads.

It goes without saying (or ought to) that any drummer worth his salt will have his own tool kit with the sort of tools appropriate to effecting minor repairs on drum equipment, and also a reasonable supply of spare parts — wing nuts, cymbal felts, tensioning rods and the like. This is not a luxury, you really must see it as essential, and you can get some ideas for what to carry with you on page 116 of this very book.

Incidentally, I don't want to appear to be leaving those who play electronic drums out of this conversation, or those who have a couple of pads added to their acoustic kit; but the fact of the matter is that electronic drums are probably more reliable (physically, at least), and there isn't much to go wrong with them that could be attended to on stage anyway. Having said that, the plugs and sockets by which the pads are connected are the most obvious source of problems, and once again, as a confidence-builder, these should be regularly checked.

## SETTING UP

It's not too handy having a bass drum that walks away from you while you're playing, or cymbal stands that seem to want to join the audience. Apart from the embarrassment and general mirth this produces, it's got to be somewhat of a hindrance to positive playing. Given the primary function of a drummer is that of time-keeper, any distractions resulting from using unstable gear, or from even worrying about it, is bound to be reflected in his or her accuracy. Recent developments in bass drum spur design have meant that modern drums show far less tendency to 'creep' than used to be the case; however, it does still occur, especially among those with a harder drumming style.

There are a number of ways of overcoming bass drum creep, from laying stone monoliths in front of or inside the drum, to nailing or screwing it down. However, if you prefer a more elegant method, how about getting a large sheet of plywood and screwing wooden blocks or 'stops' to it in all the relevant places, so that the entire kit can be held in position. The idea could be extended to marking this wooden base with the relative positions of all the drums and stands, making setting up much quicker and easier, and guaranteeing everything being in the right position, even if set up by someone else. It also helps when you arrive at a gig to be able to lay this base down in order to decide the best position for your kit, or whether it'll fit in the broom cupboard everyone seems to expect you to play in. If the size of the base is likely to be a problem, it could easily be divided up and hinged so that it folds up, or simply made in two halves — in this sort of size, it should prove no problem for the average Ford Tranny or whatever. Its use should cut down dramatically on setting-up time, and alleviate completely any worries about the dreaded creep — a confidence booster for any drummer.

To sum up the equipment aspect of stage confidence: however humble your kit may be, keep it in as good a condition as possible; keep as many spares for it as you can afford; give yourself time to handle any problems prior to the gig; and try to expand your knowledge of all the equipment and techniques involved in playing with a band. If you take note of these basic guidelines, all you'll have to worry about is you. Mind you, that still leaves plenty to worry about...

## SEEING AND HEARING

As has already been mentioned, not being able to hear everything that's going on often stems from inadequate sound checking, and though it's no excuse for losing time, it is quite easy to lose your place in a song. Having an adequate monitoring system is clearly essential for all but the smallest gigs, and for the purposes of this article, we'll assume that this is the case, because nothing, but nothing is capable of reducing you to a gibbering wreck quite like the panic that comes over you when the gig's started and you realise that you can't hear a bloody thing, and the rest of the band seem oblivious to your problems. Don't leave it for the guitarist or sound guy to sort it out for you; familiarise yourself with the basic technicalities, so that if there's a problem, you know how to deal with it. Your confidence can only be improved if you don't feel that that side of things is totally out of your hands.

As regards seeing, it should be obvious that it's the interaction of a group of musicians working together, playing the same song on the same stage, that gives a live performance that spark of magic. Because of this, it is essential that you are able to see what's going on as well as hear it. Now, though this needn't be taken to the extreme of the guitarist, facing the drummer and waggling his arse at the crowd style of head down, no nonsense,

mindless metal school of music, it does necessitate good visual contact between members of a band. Quite clearly in the case of the drummer, good communication with the bass player is essential, but given some of the current musical styles, where the entire song is built around a beat, being able to clock all the band and have them see you, should also be considered when placing yourself on stage.

I hope I've made it clear that confidence is not purely derived from a faith in your own ability. Sure, that's perhaps the most important factor, but any pursuit which involves reliance on other people and a dependence on equipment, inevitably leads to worry, doubts and nervousness. Sort these things out by anticipating problems before they occur, and you're half way there.

## 2. RISK CONTROL

If, as a member of a band, you were to stop and consider the potential for disaster to strike at the average gig, you could be excused for never setting foot out of the bedroom or garage where your ideas for stardom first took root.

Acoustic drummers, of course, can console themselves with the fact that their performance, at least, is not reliant on the constant flow of well-ordered electrons through cable and circuit board — unless they happen to be miked up through the PA system. Unfortunately, audiences are notoriously even-handed in their derision of a band experiencing 'technical difficulties': the fact that the guitarist has just had a brief misunderstanding with the mains supply, and turned his strings into a sort of extension of the national grid, tends to reflect equally on the other members of a band, providing a distraction which no amount of drum soloing can overcome.

At the risk of resorting to the cliché and the stereotype, it is relatively easy to chart the progress (or lack of) of the average band playing the average gig...

Six-thirty marks the already 'an hour late' point when the respective members of our hypothetical band The Plumber's Mates From Hell begin to drift, one by one, into the bass guitarist's bedroom which has acted as 'temporary' gear store for the last two years. Their scarcely concealed excitement is punctuated only by outrageous claims for the previous evening's level of alcohol consumption, and Spike the guitarist's seemingly effortless ability to expel air at will, following his over-indulgence at the Indian takeaway that same evening. This evening's gig at the Rat And Screwdriver, has been eagerly awaited since their previous performance — now some two months ago — and their preparation for it has extended to all areas except those which will in fact go wrong.

By carefully carrying the equipment down the stairs, through the hall, out of the front door, and into the van, casualties are kept down to a minimum three lumps of plaster, part of a door frame and a half dozen skinned knuckles. The band's first real mistake only coming to light when the van is fully loaded and Pecker, the keyboard player, remembers they haven't checked to see if the ageing and recalcitrant Transit will actually start. In the event, it amazes everyone by firing first time, but soon adopts its more traditional role as the object of everyone's scorn by immediately dying, and stubbornly refusing all attempts at revival. The following hour sees a convoy of three cars borrowed from various sources, loaded to capacity with equipment and bodies, trundling down the road in search of the evening's venue.

The arrival at the pub, though somewhat overdue, is in no one's opinion worthy of the landlord's completely stone-faced reception, or, indeed, of the insistence of the landlady that the jukebox remain on during the later sound check.

The pub itself is a tribute to fibreglass and modern plastics. Built all of three years ago, it features low ceilings, artificial beams and exposed brick walls built at odd angles and sectioning off supposedly 'intimate' little areas where one can be justifiably forced into the company of unwilling members of the opposite sex. From an acoustic point of view, it's a nightmare — a fact that the band seems oblivious of.

The venue is already half-filled with leering punters while the band are still in the process of wheeling in the gear, and no outward show of aloofness can conceal their irritation at the unbridled barrage of abuse from a particularly vociferous group of youths lounging against the bar. The band's early efforts to establish a coherent sound, and the resultant howls of feedback, are of course nothing to endear them to the already hostile management and audience. And when Fyodor, their drummer (so named because of the pocket Dostoyevski always included in his hardware case, to read in those quiet off-stage moments), starts to limber up with repeated and half-finished rolls around the toms, the audience's hackles assume a decidedly vertical aspect.

All this has been put behind them, however, when they take the stage an hour later, but it is unfortunately soon replaced by equal consternation at the uniformly appalling sound which greets them as the opening bars of the first number are struck.

What they've never been able to understand is why, when practising in a bedroom, everything sounds pretty wonderful — all the instruments fusing together, the sound coherent and full. Whereas on stage, that same sound varies between the flattering and chaotic, with tonight's performance falling miserably into the latter category. Fyodor, in particular, frequently has trouble believing that Sprout, the bass guitarist, actually has his amp switched on whenever they're on stage together. And though dimly aware of a special 'rapport' they are supposed to have formed (through an interview with Steve Gadd he once read), he hasn't quite worked out how this was possible, given his complete inability to hear his colleague's efforts.

The band were similarly aware of the existence of monitor systems, but had assumed these would arrive at the same stage in their career as black limos and women waiting to 'congratulate' them after a gig. They do make a token gesture towards mixing, but this usually takes the form of Sprout deciding his guitar can't quite be heard, and surreptitiously nudging his volume control up another notch. The rest of the band, sensing an imbalance, follow suit almost immediately, preserving their relative levels perfectly as the overall volume rises...

As the first number limps on to an inglorious end, and the band turn to look at each other, a kind of 'between song' post mortem ensues, and out of this, an argument, giving the audience an opportunity to witness a band's disintegration 'live on stage'. Good sense prevails, however, and twenty minutes later, the band has reformed.

Sadly, the audience has left..

An extreme example? Maybe. But there can be few people who've ever trod the boards as a member of a band that won't have found something in this little narrative that rings a familiar bell. But if this is the case, what's to be done?

Improving your on-stage listening environment obviously demands the use of some kind of monitoring equipment for all but the smallest gigs. Given the traditional band line-up, the drummer in many ways is in the most vulnerable position in terms of having the sound of the other instruments pass him by. Placed at the back of the stage, he frequently finds himself in line with, and in some cases behind the back-line

amplification of the other instruments. This, given the sound projecting capabilities of most speaker designs, places him in what is probably the worst position in the entire venue from a sound point of view — audience included.

It is possibly the popular concept of the role of a drummer — that of providing a back beat — which has ended up with him being placed literally at the back. The fact that much modern music is built round a beat, seems to have escaped everyone's attention when it comes to positioning instruments on stage. And quite apart from the visual aspect of a drummer providing a centre point for an audience's attention, it would seem a wholly more sensible idea for the rest of a band to be in contact with the person providing the rhythmic structure which holds the whole thing together.

Unlike the very directional properties which characterise speaker systems, the sound of an acoustic drum kit tends to be omni-directional — that is, coming out at all angles from the kit. So, with the drums further out front, you'll be seen and be able to see, and be heard, and be able to hear. None of which should be done for reasons of self-interest, but merely out of the need to give a more coherent structure to the band's sound.

This, if you think about it, is one of the many reasons many people experience difficulties in crossing over from a rehearsing to a gig situation, nervousness apart. Most bands tend to practise in smallish rooms — 'in the round', in other words, with the musicians forming a circle. In this position, everyone can be seen and heard. Straighten out that circle, put it on a stage, and the problems being.

If, for some reason, it proves impractical or impossible for the drums to be brought forward a little, there are a couple of other tricks which can be employed to help out the audibility side of a performance before we have to take recourse to monitor systems. One of these relies on the properties of low frequency sound — you know, that deep, rumbling noise the bass guitarist is responsible for (at least, the musical part of the deep, rumbling noise he's responsible for). Because low frequencies tend not to be very directional, it is really much less critical where the bass stack is positioned on stage. And this being the case, there is no reason why it cannot therefore be angled more towards the drummer, or better still, positioned behind, though perhaps a little to one side of him. This would obviously mean that the drummer is first in line to the bass's outpourings, which should mean that the mythical 'rapport' between these two doyens of the rhythm section is at least unimpeded by sound problems. And before any bass guitarists out there start to wail about their sound being obscured by the occupant of the drum stool — it won't be. Such obstacles, whatever their girth, are more or less transparent to low frequency sound.

There could be problems if the bass person in question favours a lot of 'top end' for various slapping techniques, as this would, to some extent, be absorbed or deflected by obstacles put in its way. But usually, bass players who go for this style of playing have a separate speaker cabinet for high frequencies (a 2x10″, for example), and this could be left in its normal position. In any case, I'm not suggesting for a moment that the bass speaker is totally obscured by the writhing bulk of the drummer, merely that it is positioned with him or her in mind.

Similarly, the guitarist's or keyboard player's speakers could often be more thoughtfully placed, particularly if these comprise two or more cabinets. This would allow one to be positioned more for the benefit of the drummer, though again, this clearly has to be kept within reason. Additionally, angling the PA speakers in a

little could be of benefit to the whole band when monitor speakers are not available; but great care should be taken here, given the likelihood of feedback problems from microphones. Remember, nothing in the known universe is guaranteed to have an audience wanting to drink bleach quite like the effects of prolonged howls of feedback.

Whilst on this subject, and bearing in mind what I have said about bringing the drums in a little, care should be taken to ensure that drums are positioned as far as possible out of the pick-up field of microphones — especially that of the lead vocalist. Drums and cymbals (particularly the latter), can play havoc with a singer's performance (vocal performance, that is) if they are allowed to clutter up the PA sound — this often being the only point of reference when monitor speakers are not being used.

For many bands on the road, one of the major bogeys (colonel bogeys?) of their on-stage performance is that of sound bouncing off hard, solid walls, both in front of and behind the stage. This can have a devastating effect on timing, particularly for drummers, since what you end up hearing is that which you played a few milliseconds earlier. Add to this the direct and reflected sound of other instruments, and you begin to realise that 'pea souper' is not a term which need be restricted to describing 19th Century London fog.

Solutions to the problem unfortunately don't come easy, particularly when it comes to sound reflected off the front walls. This is because what is required is some form of damping, and whilst this need take no more elaborate a form than a heavy cloth or sheet, convincing a landlord or club owner of the aesthetic value of having your grandfather's old army blanket pinned to the wall, is seldom easy. Things may perhaps be easier with a length of tastefully coloured velvet curtain, but I doubt it. The best you can really do is 'angle' the sound away from hard, flat walls, so that it is absorbed by whatever soft furnishings the room possesses, or is reflected away from the stage.

The rear wall is usually easier to deal with, and damping here can in fact also improve matters in terms of the front wall reflections. What makes it an easier problem to solve, is that it is a much more feasible proposition for a band to hang a heavy sheet behind them, particularly if it is emblazoned with their name or moniker. This, apart from helping to burn into an audience's brain just who they're listening to, makes it far easier for an intractable landlord to see the validity of the idea.

Acoustically, it can make the difference between victory and defeat in a performance — particularly for a drummer. This is again because of the omni-directional characteristics of a drum kit's sound, part of which would re-present itself to the drummer's ears after being reflected off the rear wall — which clearly is not going to do much for anybody's timing. With some means of absorbing these reflections, however, the drummer is left with the uncluttered, 'first time round' sound he or she knows and loves.

One final point on this subject, and this again concerns reflected sound at the front of the stage. Don't forget that the way things sound when a room is empty of people, will be totally different to the sound when the audience arrives (if you're lucky enough to have one). Humans have a wonderful ability to 'mop up' a lot of those nasty reflections floating around a room, without ever realising they're doing it. In fact it is quite often the case that the acoustics you have cursed during a sound check, have dramatically improved by the time you come to take the stage, so in a way you've got an audience on your side, even though they may be hating what you play.

However, one other effect that massed human beings have on acoustics should also be taken into account at this stage, and that is their dampening of high frequencies. Now, though it is true to say that the treble frequencies will probably sound a lot more damped from your position on the stage than they do from the audience's stand-point, this is still something which you should be aware of. A friend with a good ear placed in the audience can be invaluable in this respect, and is probably the best way of achieving anything like a consistent sound from gig to gig.

It seems that musicians are basically creatures of habit, and as such, it is easy to assume that because each member of a band sets up his gear in a certain position at every gig, that is the position which it has to be set up in. Don't be afraid to experiment. Positioning of drums and equipment is all-important in terms of achieving a balanced sound, but there are no hard and fast rules. All that is important, is that given the drummer's central role as time-keeper, he, above all others has to be heard by everyone in the band. This, besides creating a direct line of communication between him and each musician, also establishes him as an intermediary between the other musicians. I suppose you could view it as a sort of telephone exchange, with the drummer at the centre, keeping the whole functioning.

Of course, all of the foregoing information is applicable only to bands without monitoring or a full PA system, because with this sort of equipment most of these problems simply don't arise. With a guy on the mixing desk at the back of the room, it is possible to tailor the sound to suit the acoustic environment of the audience and that of the band quite separately, and clearly — this is the end towards which most bands should be working. Maintaining control over your acoustic environment, is not merely desirable, it is essential for any musicians serious about what they're doing, and should therefore be put high on the list of priorities of any aspiring band.

Speaking of which, what of The Plumber's Mates From Hell? Well, unbeknown to them, in the audience that evening are the talent scouts for six major record companies. And following the gig, the band are besieged with offers of recording contracts, together with huge advances running into tens of thousands of pounds. Unfortunately, just as they are deciding which of the companies they will have to disappoint, Fyodor's alarm clock rings...

## Fright Night

As every artist knows, when you are in front of an audience and your performance has to be perfect, your body is gripped with an unreasonable and totally irrational anxiety that transforms you from a perfectly competent drummer in the rehearsal studio, into a ham-fisted wreck on stage. So what is it that creates this distressing Jeckyl & Hopeless Hyde scenario?

Basically, there are two main culprits here: excitement and nerves. The first tends to push up the tempo and creates an urgent desire to impress the audience — who needs subtlety when you can have speed, noise and sweat? The second is far more significant, and much more difficult to suppress; nerves cause serious angst, which in turn restricts your ability to play. This is most noticeable when you've rehearsed a particular move or style until it's ingrained in your mind. You find it simple and almost automatic, until you come to premier it on stage and suddenly it's gone.

Ironically, nerves are quite natural and, in many ways, vital to a good performance. They keep you aware of the dangers of bad

playing and alert you to the consequences of making mistakes. Nervousness is caused by the presumption of inferiority. The confidence you develop through practice and experience is eaten away by a subconscious pessimism. These feelings are largely unfounded, since most members of the audience will be quite unaware of a drummer's talents, or lack of them. What they will notice, however, is a lack of confidence and an insistence on playing and failing unnecessary moves. Concentrate more on improving the song, or making people dance and tap their feet.

Even the greatest drummers suffer from nerves; the only reason you don't notice this is because experience has taught them to hide it. They have confronted the problem head-on, they've accepted that their practice will always be superior to their live work. However, as they practise more, the standard of both will improve. Developing your skills is a very, very slow process. If you're working on new ideas, introduce them to your live show slowly. Try them first at gigs where you have more freedom and the pressure is lower. Think back to the days when you fist started playing, and how long it took to play a basic beat with confidence; it's the same with new styles and ideas. The fact that you're a competent drummer doesn't mean that your brain can absorb new activities any quicker than when you started. Everything takes time.

How nervous you are and how well you play can vary enormously from gig to gig. There is no easy explanation for this, but maintaining a good diet and getting plenty of sleep can only improve your overall standard of playing. A major factor in sustaining a constant level of performance is learning to breathe properly. I'm sure some of the symptoms of my early playing will be familiar to you. I'd launch into drum fills at breakneck speed, holding my breath all the way through, only to emerge at the

○ **Excitement and nerves: sweat and angst**

other end completely out of breath and energy. When playing, it's important to keep your breathing steady and deep.

Outside influences can also play a big part in your confidence levels. When playing live, for instance, the sound of your kit will vary greatly from venue to venue.

This is simply another obstacle you must accept and overcome; learn to work within the parameters set for you, and never use them as an excuse for bad playing.

Here's a quick checklist of ways to deal with the problems you may face:

★ *Always warm up before you play.*

★ *Run through your live set in your mind before gigs; associate the name of each song with the tempo and feel.*

★ *Don't try to play everything you know at every gig. Introduce new 'tricks' gradually.*

★ *Breathe deeply before and throughout the gig. This will give you a clear head and much more stamina.*

★ *Relaxation and concentration. Your mental effort should be split 50/50 between the two.*

Accept that your live playing standards will differ from those in rehearsal. Learn to live with this, and use it as an incentive to practice harder and improve both sides of your drumming.

Remember, nerves are never going to go away, and moreover are an essential part of the buzz achieved from live performance. If however you are one of those rare people who never suffer from nerves, I hope you realise how lucky you are.

## Be Prepared

I've always been a strong advocate of prophylactics when it comes to drums and accessories, and it's actually nothing to do with condoms, just a perfectly reasonable philosophy which dictates that it's better to thoroughly inspect your gear from time to time rather than wait until it lets you down. It's preventative medicine, a bit like an MOT really.

Invariably, it's the smallest of components which go wrong, and those should always be checked carefully. Split-pins and grub screws have an annoying tendency to fall out, while rivets are prone to loosening. Those can be replaced with siliconised, aircraft-type lock nuts, and stripped threads can be re-tapped. I once managed to replace a broken nylon link on my hi-hats, during a gig, with a doubled-over bass drum strap. I liked it so much, I still use it.

Sod's law decrees that anything that can go wrong will go wrong, so it's in your interest to have some sort of first aid kit stashed away in your trap case. I've carried one around for years, neatly packed in an old metal biscuit tin. It's become a dented a great deal due to stands and things being bashed into it, but its contents have remained intact. Unfortunately, the see-through plastic drawer units you can get from DIY stores are useless; they're the ideal size but break far too easily. My tin is compartmentalised and contains the following collection of essentials:

**1.** *A couple of leather straps and spare expansion springs for foot pedals.*

**2.** *A couple of tilter sleeves, some polythene tubing, felt washers, and wing-nuts for cymbal stands.*

**3.** *Tensioners for toms, snare and bass drum.*

**4.** *A claw.*

**5.** *A spare bass drum beater.*

**6.** *A cheap hi-hat clutch.*

**7.** *A tool with different Allen keys.*

**8.** *A handful of nuts, bolts, and different sized washers.*

**9.** *Assorted self-tapping screws.*

**10.** *A leather bass drum patch.*

**11.** *A few long nails to mend pedals.*

**12.** *Some string.*

**13.** *A single-edged razor blade.*

**14.** *Plastic strips for attaching snares.*

**15.** *A tube of Vaseline.*

**16.** *A couple of adjustable hose-clips (so I can still use a stand even if the height adjustment screw strips).*

**17.** *A pair of pliers.*

**18.** *A stubby screwdriver.*

**19.** *Some Superglue.*

**20.** *And should all else fail, a few yards of gaffer tape wrapped round a pencil.*

I have a sticky label on my biscuit tin that lists exactly what's inside. But

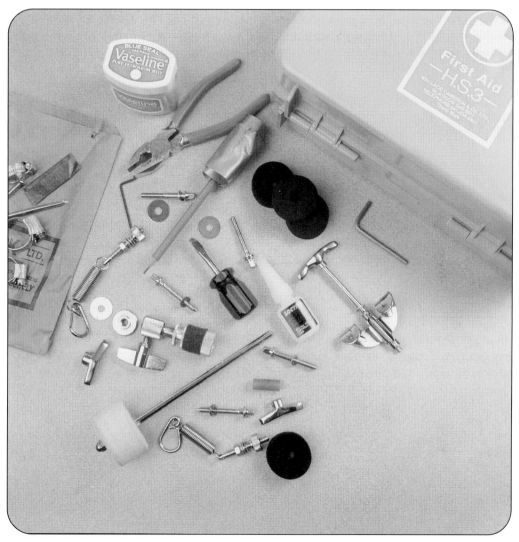

⊙ **Any drummer worth his salt will have his own tool kit with tools for minor repairs**

remember, for this first aid kit to work, anything you use must be replaced as soon as possible.

What I'm recommending here is a spot of thoughtful preventative medicine, rather like checking your heads before a gig to see if they're likely to break. (A good tip on this score is to rotate your bass drum head occasionally to minimise wear; although this will only work if your beater doesn't hit dead centre of the drum.)

Breaking heads is always a problem, and any gigging drummer should at least have spares for the ultra-essential snare and bass drum.

Of course, even if you have spares when disaster strikes, you'll have to fit them in the middle of a gig, and it's impossible to do so without stopping. But help is at hand, for the snare at least.

Order yourself a 15″ Remo PTS pre-tuned head, which can be simply taped over a broken batter head and the drum hoop and tensioners. It's a quick job to rip away the broken film and get on with the show. A 14″ PTS will work too, but obviously it takes longer to undo the tensioners and remove the rim.

While I'm on the subject, I use another piece of preventative medicine on my hands. Painful experience has shown me exactly where my hands will blister and bleed, so instead of waiting for the damage to be done, I put a small piece of spongy adhesive plaster made by Johnson & Johnson in the crucial places. It ain't macho, but it does mean I can play hard every day without problems.

# chapter 11
## In Vogue

"Fa-fa-fa-fa-fashion!" squawked David Bowie and his funny sounding mates. "Fashion! Turn to the left! Fashion! Turn to the right!" And that's exactly what we do, as if on cue. Drummers are as susceptible to fashion as anyone else. The drumming community has seen many to-be-mourned haircuts through the years, but it is amongst the drums and the cymbals et al that fashion has rampaged mercilessly, though that design classic, the T-shirt and jeans, remains untouchable. Aside from the giant steps that the actual technology of building drums took in the Seventies — bigger shells, sturdier stands — drums and drumming have seen as much wilful fashion as spring in Paris or Milan. And this is not to say that manufacturing has not, or does not improve — it just gets better and better, the effects of which are felt most keenly on the budget end of the market where product is unimaginably fine. I'm not complaining, not really, but I do have a beef, and what brought it to mind was the arrival within the same month on the scene of tiny single lugs and more cymbals that 'have a jazzy tone but are suitable for rock'. I mean, pur-leaze! I bought the last lot of gear that fitted those requirements, I can't go through all this again, I feel like I'm being played for a sucker.

And maybe I am. A sucker. As a for instance, lugs have gone up and down: five years ago we all had to have single tension lugs, as they spread out the stress (or something — I'm just a punter, how am I supposed to know really? It's not like I have a lab at home to run tests on the latest gear), but now we all need tiny lugs that hardly impede the shell at all, thus allowing the shell to ring free blah, blah, blah... What's going on? Maybe the clue is in what Pearl did some years ago to the Export kit — all of a sudden single piece lugs were in, but arse! they'd been caught out, so what did they do? They put cosmetic 'single' lugs on the kit, pieces of beautifully chromed metal bridging the gap between the suddenly unfashionable tension lugs they had there in the first place. While this is obviously not on the scale of Coke changing their recipe and then changing it back and calling it Coke Classic, it still seems, well, weird. Surely what we want from drum manufacturers is the pursuit of excellence at all times, the best sound for our pound, and surely that is always what we get. Don't think I'm trying to insinuate a stitch up, but where else can we buy the gear?

Tom sizes are another example. Power toms they were called, and for a while you couldn't move for them; great big things, and we bought them by the ton. Power toms. Then of course we didn't want power toms any more. Oh no, what we wanted was a fusion kit. Who asked us? I'm sure we were asked, but we were all so certain about the power toms a minute ago, and anyway Vinnie (or Whoever) uses one.

Certainly at the budget end things get very confusing, although I've always felt that a budget kit is only as good as the heads you put on it (in other words they can be pretty good), and if you're starting out you're more likely to be looking for the kit that Whoever uses — the advertising, endorsing and all is pretty seductive. And subtle, especially the fusion kit and its buddies.

The fusion kit (and I bought one... two in fact — a budget one, and then I upgraded, so I speak from a position of experience) has all sorts of subtle and clever associations that come with it for free. Fusion... Now I don't play fusion, not by any stretch of the imagination, nor do I play fusion-esque; I get told to shut up or worse. But I bought a fusion kit. Why? i. It fits in the car more easily than the Power toms of yore (oh yes I fell for that one too). And ii. the name. Fusion. What does that say to you? It says to me great players, grrrreat drummers who I can only hope to dream of emulating, and one easy way to do that is to play kits like theirs. It's the same thing as the cymbals that have all the jazz sensibilities but are suitable for rock etc. etc. blah blah... You see, rock music is not really the hardest thing to do in terms of drumming — though grrrreat rock drumming is like a haiku: perfect, untouchable, rounded, a thing of beauty — but jazz is where the playing's at.

It's difficult to do at all, let alone well, and if you want to sound just like Art or Max or Tony or Whoever (him again) while you belt out 'The Birdy Song' in the Dog and Duck, what you need is a jazz cymbal of course. Though if you actually had one, the band would complain about the noise. So what you get is a jazz cymbal that can be used in rock music — cake and eat it. And not only that, but they can sell it to you the other way round all over again in a couple of years time! I'm not knocking any of these products, they are all fabulous — I am the person who is buying this stuff for these very reasons, and it's that that really annoys me. It's not just me either; if I was the only sucker around here then I doubt that they would be making a cymbal or bass drum just for me. Charlie Watts springs to mind as someone who doesn't seem to be affected — same kit and cymbals for donkeys years; if it ain't broke etc. But then he's Charlie Watts; he's never, ever going to play 'The Birdy Song', unless someone convinced him it was about Charlie Parker.

Maybe I'm reading too much into it, but if I were starting out I wouldn't know where to begin. When my mum gave me my first snare drum, I hankered for a cymbal, and a cymbal with Z in its name was what I desired above all else. She wisely went to the other end of the alphabet and brought back an Ajax, which sadly will never come back into fashion. Though I tell you this, and I swear it on a gallon of secret recipe alloy: if I ever make it as a drummer I will stride into whichever manufacturer's office is at my beck and call and get them to make one just like it. And you'll buy it! Ha ha, and then who will be the sucker..? Ha ha ha ha!

# chapter 12
## School Daze

## One

In the days before the acoustic Vs electronics debate, there were but two issues that the drummer needed concern himself with: the traditional or matched grip, and whether or not to take lessons. The former discussion no longer appears to generate any interest, but the latter still seems to be going strong.

Nowadays there are a lot of drum teachers available; or, to take a more cynical view, there are a lot of drum teachers around with vacancies for students. Now why should I, a self-confessed teacher of the drums, introduce this note of cynicism? Simply because I recognise that a large number of the drumming community would like to see all drum teachers made to carry a government health warning along the lines of: Taking Lessons From Self-Appointed Authorities May Be Injurious To Your Creativity.

Considering that drummers perceive themselves as being particularly individualistic, they are quick to assign a convenient stereotype to teachers. It runs as follows: a clapped-out jazzer with the obligatory four-piece red sparkle 1950s kit,

sporting a picture of a red Indian bidding farewell to his horse on the bass drum. His professional playing career came to an end circa 1963 when a fickle public transferred its affections from the Paramount Jazz Band to the Beatles. This testament to the embalmer's art gives lessons in a purpose-built teaching studio which strongly resembles a garden shed, and wherein bass drum activity has to be somewhat rationed to avoid knocking over the paraffin heater. It is strongly rumoured that this last option would result in generating considerably more excitement than the actual lesson content, which provides a staple diet of flams, paradiddles and odd numbered rolls. This teacher does not question the validity of the 26 snare drum rudiments, for he has found them to be equally applicable for Dixieland jazz, military band concerts, certain old time dances, and to accompany the comedian's funny walk during cabaret spots. (This last 'hot lick' being the triple ratamacue, for the technically minded among you.) His enthusiasm for technique is matched only by his reluctance to discuss their application to present musical styles, and a rumour persists that his teaching derives from a lack of current musical employment rather than a genuine desire to disseminate information...

While some stories regarding teachers must surely be apocryphal, there is, unfortunately, an element of truth in it all. Now, you can be sure that there is nobody more cynical of drum teachers in general than one drum teacher in particular, but I actually met the other stereotype recently. What? You haven't? Let me introduce you — ex-regimental bandsman, thirteen snare drum rudiments, no recourse to written notation, recently added a bass drum and hi-hat to the snare drum for 'a bit of fun'.

As a (presumably) musician in the 1990s, you are probably concerned with the demands of what might be termed 'new music', and how to incorporate techniques, technology and concepts to your future development. As such, you are unlikely to be much impressed with these stereotypes, although I have students of, shall we say, more mature years and conservative tastes who would not be too alarmed at the type of study I have outlined. These would be the musicians who handle commercial work for clubs, dances and functions on a strictly part-time basis, and would have little or no interest in rock, electronics, modern jazz etc., and are well suited to a more traditional lesson content.

Younger players tend to be more adventurous in their playing and often more discriminating and demanding regarding tuition. I often hear new students complaining of a previous teacher that he operated in a time warp and/or suffered from premature senile decay, or else displayed no interest in his pupil's aspirations. Both are worthy reasons for the cessation of lessons; if a teacher cannot offer you relevant experience and instruction in the areas you wish to study, then it's time to settle up and move on — you have merely encountered a mismatch.

If, on the other hand, you are unfortunate enough to have encountered the second category — the teacher with no interest in you or your development, or even in his own lesson content — it becomes harder to reconcile yourself to parting with your money, even for the 'lesson' you have just received. You will derive something from the first teacher if he is making an honest endeavour to communicate with you, but absolutely nothing from the second.

The key word to your course of study should be 'relevant'. I don't necessarily advocate that the only way to make progress in, say, modern jazz is to study exclusively with a modern jazz player. Joe Morello, who possesses surely one of the most amazing techniques of any musician playing any music, worked solely with teachers from orchestral backgrounds — notably Billy Gladstone and George Lawrence Stone. In one interview, Joe is quoted as having begged lessons from Gladstone, saying, "I want that kind of control because I can use it."

The problem with studying technical exercises is that they are often presented as non-musical exercises, ie. as ends in themselves. Rudiments can, if properly applied, give you considerable freedom in kit playing by fostering the ability to place your hands exactly where you want them to produce combinations of sounds and dynamics. If approached in this fashion, students are less likely to practise rudiments incessantly and then confine themselves to single strokes when actually performing.

If you are worried about becoming a 'rudimental clone', consider three strong rudimental players: Dave Weckl, Peter Erskine and Terry Bozzio; whatever else you may think of their playing, you wouldn't easily confuse them, would you? It has always seemed to me that British drummers are far less inclined toward formal study than their American counterparts, and yet frequently revere not only their technical expertise, but also their superior 'feel' for time playing and getting inside a particular number. However, many people maintain that these skills are innate or possibly acquired, but definitely not taught and probably impeded by any input from a teacher.

I think the standard of the 'schooled' American players proves this to be incorrect. I don't imagine anybody is going to be terribly surprised or upset when I say that the music programmes in American high school and colleges are far in advance of our own. I would suppose that these programmes account also for the high standards of private teachers in the States, since potential students know what to look for in a teacher/pupil relationship, and thus only the better teachers continue to thrive.

My experience of working with young drummers in this country who are associated with various youth orchestras, jazz ensembles etc. under the auspices of Local Education Authorities, is that they are frequently poor readers and players. This is the result of performing in an ensemble to the exclusion of studying the instrument separately. The jazz players, strangely enough, are often the poorest; their sense of time and swing is often so at odds with the rest of the ensemble that they would have difficulty moving an audience stricken by diarrhoea and supplied with running shoes!

Now, apart from a justified fear of being exploited by some unscrupulous teacher, what else inhibits a serious study of the drums? Well, one very good reason must be the relative ease of playing one associates with the instrument — no melody or harmony, no problems with embouchure, fingering, intonation, tone (you can tune them, can't you?), all serve to make the drum kit easy to play by ear. Sooner or later you begin to realise that you have reached a plateau. As time passes, it also becomes increasingly harder to subject yourself to lessons — because without them, you've

been enjoying yourself, right? Who, at this stage of his or her career needs to be scrutinised and told (however gently) that it's really not that good?

Another reason often expressed by drummers is the fear of being moulded into a carbon copy of the teacher, thereby losing spontaneity, individual creativity, expression, and any ability to redefine the boundaries of drumming. This is not just a phenomenon of the rock generation, by the way; the small group of be-bop jazz drummers of the late 1940s and 1950s rejected the drum charts of the big swing bands in favour of spontaneity, and were apt to reply to the (even then) perennial question of reading music, "Not enough to hurt my playing."

Although it was to become fashionable to study with 'name' drummers, the primary concern was to absorb a certain ethos from these players, and to emulate their mental approach to the instrument rather than to attempt to physically imitate their style. Vibist Gary Burton is quoted as having said, "It is possible to be a drummer based primarily on technique and not so much on musicality," but nobody should assume that all lessons with all teachers will ignore this musicality.

A central issue where taking lessons is concerned is the question of learning to read music — anathema to so many drummers, and probably the major reason for avoiding study. You would be amazed at how many people ring me out of the blue just to let me know what they can already do and why they don't need lessons that involve music reading, and/or to ask if they can come round to the studio just to ask a few general questions or to glean information about a particular technique — anything so long as it's not called a lesson and doesn't involve written notation. There was a time when, being an obliging sort of chap, I used to work hard at tuition without referring to the 'tadpoles on the telephone wires' for those who insisted on it. I now refuse point blank to do it for the following reasons:

**1.** *With the help of a good teacher, reading music is easy, the only requirement being an ability on the part of the student to count as far as four. If you can't do that already, I would assume you're using this page for something other than reading matter.*

**2.** *People who insisted on learning new techniques solely by ear were in the habit of leaving the studio, walking five yards down the path, and then returning to ask to hear it again... and again... and again... It has been useful in clearing snow away from the door, but tends on those occasions to make the studio cold — there is no other useful purpose. Written notation does not yield up every nuance involved in playing, but it's an effective mnemonic (Greek for a bloody good reminder).*

**3**. *You can continue to practise at home with or without a drum kit; mental practice from a written score is valuable in analysing form and shape of a piece, and can keep you gainfully occupied at times when family and neighbours dictate that you are unable to physically practise.*

**4**. *You can check your progress by working from a set book (you do want to progress, don't you?). That increases your motivation and makes lessons more enjoyable for me too.*

**5.** *You will become more innovative in your playing, using more variations and juxtapositions of ideas, simply because you will be better able to visualise what you are playing, and how it may be modified or embellished. Technique is the*

*tool, not the master, and you should use it towards control and mastery — the only real freedom.*

**6.** *There are no harmful side effects, such as losing the ability to improvise — you may have noticed that great orators are not, as a rule, illiterate.*

**7.** *Career prospects may not increase, but they certainly won't diminish.*

**8.** *You achieve access to a wealth of drum literature, and are able to communicate more easily with other musicians and even machines.*

**9.** *Why should any of us want to demean our chosen instrument by denying the use of a well established system of notation? Too much of that and we'll be back to the old cracks of 'four musicians and a drummer'.*

Now let's put some of the onus regarding drum tuition on you. The most important decisions can only be made by you — whether or not to study, in what specific field, and with whom. I will however offer some advice to help you.

If you feel you are in a rut and not progressing (and still not having Top Five hits), you need to be exposed to something new — lessons may facilitate this. Once you have decided where the focus of your attention is to be directed, check out the available teachers. Be sure that anyone you select at least feels able to work with you towards achieving your goal. You will need at this stage to outline as fully as possible what you require in terms of skills and facilities. On both counts, be realistic. Don't, for example, expect to master 'systems' music if you can't already read music and do not possess a fair degree of co-ordination and independence. If you wish to work exclusively with MIDI and recording equipment, be prepared to travel.

You should look for, and ideally find, a teacher who will not only give you an improved technique, but also an increased awareness of music in general, and the opportunities to develop concepts which will enable you to find your own individual voice as a musician.

I believe that you can play anything that you can conceptualise. To do that, you need to understand, so ask questions when you don't. If you continue not to understand, then the learning process is breaking down. Don't be a passive pupil; the teaching process is two-way, and you must contribute if you want it to be successful. Your teacher should explain the purpose of each and every lesson (even if it is only revision), and his teaching and the material he uses (books, tapes etc.) should proceed logically towards set objectives. You should, in the first instance, allow him to proceed to see if his methods are effective.

Expect to do new things in a lesson. There is little point in spending money to continually trot out what you can already do, or in going along to have your ego massaged. Don't be too proud to work from time to time on some of the basics as regards relaxation, movement, posture, grips and strokes — it's not always a ploy to sell extra lessons.

Don't go to lessons where the teacher continually demonstrates his ability to play solos — real drum clinics feature more renowned players. Don't go to teachers whose stock-in-trade is constant criticism of other teachers and players; it's a cover for their deficiencies. Avoid 'easy-learn', 'non-reading', 'non-rudimental', 'non-technical' methods — you've found a non-teacher.

Don't assume that a teacher is not going to be interested in your sphere of music; one particular delight in our studio was working with a student and a tape he had brought in entitled *The Hits Of 1929*, and the particular number 'I Want To Linger Longer In Virginia' (there must be a suitable response to that which I haven't yet come up with). Don't tolerate rudeness or belligerence — they are rarely productive. But above all, don't put up with indifference. Do determine the success of your pupil/teacher relationship, and above all — have fun!

As for me, I'm off to the studio to lure some more hapless students into accompanying Sousa marches on the radiogram while I give that red sparkle an extra polish...

## Two

Okay, so in Part One hopefully you picked up some useful tips when it comes to selecting and dealing with drum tutors. But what if you yourself want to teach? Read on...

Before outlining how you might establish a thriving drum tuition business (and yes, I do know it's considered more polite to refer to it as a 'practice' rather than a business), let's first consider why you want to teach. Extra money (naturally), a degree of prestige, and the prospect of increased commercial work are all good enough reasons and are quite capable of being realised if you are successful. But they need to be offset with a real desire to impart knowledge to your pupils and, of course, the necessary skills to do so. The skills you will need are as follows:

**1.** *A certain prowess as a musician.*

**2.** *An ability to teach, by which I mean the personality needed to effectively communicate ideas and practices.*

○ A drum clinic at the Musicians' Institute in London: a popular and effective way to learn

**3.** *The business acumen needed to deal with people and money over a continued period.*

Here, I would like to concentrate on your present abilities and how they can be adapted for a teaching career, before dealing with expanding your facilities and how to go about marketing them.

As a musician, you should be experienced and competent in whatever field you elect to teach in. You may notice that I use the word 'musician' rather than 'drummer'; this is because your knowledge should extend to an understanding of the music you are playing, and how you are contributing towards it, rather than just considering the role of the drums in isolation.

This doesn't mean that you need to be especially well versed in chord progressions, melody, harmony etc., but you should be able to pick out the changes in a number by ear, and also be able to relate ideas on how to accommodate them. The musical drummer should be aware of song forms such as AABA, ABAC, and the number of bars contained within them, and be able to pass on even to complete beginners how these can be enhanced by using different tone colours, dynamics, feels and rhythms, and slight shifts in tempos. This will offer an early opportunity for your pupils to become involved in creativity, phrasing, improvisation and expression, as opposed to merely bashing out a beat. There is, by the way, a more complicated song form called ABACAB, which I have always thought would be a good title for a song...

This ear-training, or musicalogical approach to playing should become one of your greatest strengths in helping another player towards the interpretation of a particular piece. You should extend it to at least a rudimentary analysis of what other musicians are attempting within a common framework, and how the drummer should be interacting with them.

If you play keyboards or guitar, you could perhaps demonstrate some of these ideas during your lessons, but don't be dismayed if you can't — you have the world's finest musicians readily available on recordings to do the job for you. To better understand the role of melodic instruments, try experimenting with the high, middle and low pitched sounds on the drum kit, and emulating tunes and melodic solos. You will not be able to play the actual melodies, but you should be able to appreciate their shape, form and rhythms. This becomes especially useful if you use effects such as reverb and delay and wish to phrase accordingly.

Developing musical appreciation is probably the greatest gift you can give to your pupils, whatever their level of ability, but don't attempt to over-analyse. Music is like a living organism in as much that an undue amount of dissection will render it lifeless, so use these opportunities instead to convey enthusiasm for the instrument and the music, and to encourage the development of valuable concepts in your pupils which will continue to bring that 'extra something' to their performances.

You will also, in my view, need to be a fluent reader of drum music, and be well versed in musical technology — it's permissible to call quavers eighth notes but not to mistake them for a cheese flavoured snack! It is much easier to communicate ideas by recourse to a written score than by shouting "now!" at the top of your voice every time you want pupils to hit a backbeat, or contending that a Dave Weckl fill proceeds along the lines of "a-rum-ti-tiddly-bumbly bum, dingly-ding-dong,

splash-bash-blat-splat!" Apart from the inherent danger of being committed to an institution where you won't be allowed to play with pointed instruments, you run the immediate risk of making a fool of yourself in the eyes of your pupils and, probably much worse, attempting to make fools of them by failing in your duty to properly equip them in basic theory.

A proper study of the instrument involves the study of its notation and will provide your lessons with form and substance. It will allow you to work from standard drum method literature towards making real progress with your pupils, and will also supply them with the necessary tools to make transcriptions from recordings and to develop your own writing skills.

As regards technique on the kit, we all have our deficiencies and need to be aware of them. Years of playing jazz and fusion have left me with a preference for setting up figures commencing with my left hand. This doesn't adapt very readily to playing sixteenth notes around the kit and has to be amended when teaching in the rock idiom.

In addition to being aware of limitations and personal habits, you should also freely confess them and demonstrate how they can form the basis of an individual style by determining the alternate stickings and patterns you will need to employ. An analytical mind can compensate for technical restrictions if you can use it to identify the constituent parts of a difficult technique and encourage pupils to go on to master it. A by-product of this analytical approach is that you may well find that your own playing will improve and allow you to identify your own difficulties and rectify them, thus achieving better execution of technique.

I do not, however, suggest that this two-way learning process should be a central theme of your teaching. Pupils are apt to question your musicianship if you frequently ask them to explain techniques to you, or if your response to any recordings they play to you is invariably, "...buggered if I know what the drummer's up to — must be electronics."

What you probably already have on your side is versatility. Drummers more than any other instrumentalists are usually able to play in a variety of musical settings. You are not likely to be equally adept or experienced in every conceivable style, but your musicianship should enable you to function adequately within them. This will become increasingly important when teaching; not all enquiries for your services are going to relate to 'four on the floor' playing, and you will be lucky to sustain a teaching practice based on one particular style.

In the States, there are so many good drum teachers available that many have chosen to specialise. I must admit to being chastened to read that Woody Herman's ex-drummer Sonny Igoe, a man with considerable experience both as a player and a teacher, confines his own teaching largely to brushwork and chart reading. You may be able to specialise in your chosen field — indeed, you may have no other option if your locality already boasts other established teachers — but it is more likely that, having elected to teach, expectations will be that you can work effectively within a number of varied styles.

Let's now examine your role as a teacher. You've all heard George Bernard Shaw's assertion that, "He who can, does. He who cannot, teaches." This offers proof that GBS would not have made much of a go teaching the drums — indeed, his execution of the single stroke roll drew little critical acclaim, and he seems, in fact, to have played very few gigs in his lifetime (and none at all thereafter!). What he might have done better to say is that teachers can't devote time to the teaching process

without losing some opportunities to practise what they preach.

Thus your first consideration as a teacher should be this: are you going to be available to teach? If you take on a small number of pupils, it may be possible to fit their lessons around your playing commitments; but if you want to do a lot of teaching and establish a schedule wherein you see pupils at a set time each week, you should make every effort to adhere to it and not disrupt the continuous flow of your teaching programme. Therefore you should only take on that number of pupils that you can easily accommodate, and at times when you are certain to be available. Remember that you might be a working musician and free in the daytime, but your pupils are usually available to study only during evenings and weekends.

Extend this level of organisation to your actual teaching. Prepare your lessons in advance and have all the necessary materials to hand. If pupils are paying you by the hour, don't use up precious time subjecting them to glimpses of your rear end while you search for the relevant score amongst the padding in your bass drum. You should follow a set regime in your lessons. Each should begin with a brief revision and assessment of previous work, and an introduction to what is about to be undertaken and how it relates to previously acquired skills. Set a goal and work to achieve it.

There should then follow the actual lesson, in which you will be demonstrating technique, outlining concepts and listening to, and assessing, your pupils' performances. The lesson should end with a period of freer activity for the pupil, during which he or she is able to utilise some of what has been learnt — playing to a pre-recorded tape, for example. You will need to be aware of the pacing of a lesson for it to have the maximum impact. Nobody is capable of sitting at a drum for an entire hour and executing nothing but demi-semiquaver press rolls, so plan to include a variety of challenges within a lesson which do not all involve using the same muscle group.

An ongoing, two-way conversation is productive in a lesson as long as it's relevant to the content — don't enter into long diatribes concerning your marital problems or the effects of last night's curry on your digestive tract, and don't encourage your pupils to do so either. Act at all times with honesty and integrity. Devote your full attention to your pupils — when one of them is working out to the Mahavishnu Orchestra, it is not the time to go and wash your car or to pick out likely winners from the racing pages.

Insist on good standards of work and attendance from your pupils, and work hard to equip each and every one properly and adequately. Turn pupils away rather than waste their time and money if they continually fail to make progress; it could be your fault or theirs, but you don't want, or need, a reputation for producing poor players.

You can come to occupy a rather nice position as a sort of guru to your pupils, but you must be equal to it. Offer good, sound advice on all aspects of drumming and music without lapsing into quasi-mystical pronouncements such as, "What is the time anyway?" You may be much impressed at receiving money for this posturing, but people are less impressed at having to pay for it.

Something you will quickly come to appreciate when you open your door to the Great British Public (or at least to a representative sample) is that you are — hopefully — going to come into regular, sustained contact with a wide variety of people with different experiential backgrounds and aspirations. Dealing with different personalities is something that at first should be seen as an enjoyable

challenge and something you should become increasingly confident and competent at.

You will have to adapt your teaching style to accommodate different age groups, levels of ability, musical tastes etc. — in short, to deal with different individuals and objectives. In my experience of drummers who opt to take lessons, less than 50 percent are absolute beginners, and of those, a good many are in their twenties or older. Younger pupils are often accompanied (at least in the initial stages) by parents who will often be the source of useful recommendations for further pupils. All this means that although your lesson format, content and presentation may be subject to a number of variables, one thing needs to remain a constant — you.

You must in all respects inspire confidence in everyone you deal with so that you have a very clear understanding of what you are teaching, and that they will also be able to achieve it with diligence and application. To do this, you need to confidently assess how you are presenting yourself. Don't appear at lessons in a dishevelled state or complaining of tiredness and illness. Don't appear bored or disinterested, or wander about attending to less immediate tasks. Be alert, responsive, helpful, supportive and encouraging. Smile a great deal and help pupils to relax by creating an atmosphere in which they're allowed to fail in the first instance without becoming discouraged or inhibited.

Your lesson structure plays an important part in this process. Once some basic strokes and co-ordination patterns have been mastered, you can easily devise quite impressive sounding exercises, or even construct charts to accompany recordings which the pupil enjoys. You can also write out rhythms that pupils can already play by ear. They should get a real sense of achievement from being able to perform these, and this will increase confidence and motivation, making new challenges easier for both of you to undertake.

Being able to surround your teaching with an aura of enjoyment and success is what will make you a respected and established teacher. What will make you a financial success depends, naturally, upon all of the above, but also the ability to promote and create demand for your services. And that, as they say, is another story...

# chapter 13
## Dead Men's Shoes

"We'd like you to join the band." Great words to hear — someone rates you as a player, they've got a vacancy, and who do they come to? You. Fantastic. But there could be a tiny, niggling problem. Only a tiny little one, but one that you could face for quite a while: namely, the drummer whose place you're taking, for whatever reason. Whether he's been fired or exploded leaving only a green blob on the drum stool (or 'Throne' as we're supposed to call it these days), you're up against your predecessor in many subtle ways. It's something all of us go through from time to time, and you never know quite how it's going to work out, but stepping into another drummer's place is one of the hardest things you can go through. Worst of all is joining a band who have been a fair old distance with their old drummer, rather than being a session player taking on the new job, because obviously being in a band is not like a job — it's chemistry. It's banter. It's tension. It's being the one with the car. Kenny Jones taking Keith Moon's place; Led Zep unable to carry on without Bonzo; Jack Irons picking up where Dave Abbruzzese was told to leave off... Suddenly everyone — not just the drummers as is usually the case — is looking to the drummer and whispering.

Of course the only reason I mention this is that it's something I'm having to deal with at the moment. A friend of mine's band is between drummers, and I've got enough space in my diary to fill in for a while. Groovy — time to get stuck into some proper playing. We have a lot of rehearsals planned, so with any luck I'll pick it up pretty quickly. We get to the rehearsals, the bass player marvels at my 14″ crash cymbal — "so small" (where have I heard that before?) — and while I'm limbering up he says something about me playing very quietly. And I always thought I was a noisy bastard. I boldly announce that if what I'm doing isn't what they all want, all they have to do is say so and I'll do what I can to deliver the goods, the words seeming weird and unnatural even as I say them. We blow through a tune and get from one end to the other without too much trouble. Everyone's happy. We do another two or three songs. It's only the second time through the numbers that I'm told: "What used to happen here is..." I get self conscious, nervous even, but at least I'm not the first person to have gone through this. For instance...

"So I said to Brian, what's going on? I mean he said he wanted to see me about something serious, so I thought that maybe there was a problem with a venue for one of the gigs... and then he said to me, 'The boys want you out of the band and they want Ringo instead', and I said, 'Why Ringo? I'm a much better drummer than Ringo'. And he said, 'That's just the way the boys want it'." So goes an interview with Pete Best on a (rather strange) bootleg I heard once called, not altogether inappropriately, *Piss Off Pete*. The position Ringo found himself in, though helped by their staggering, unimaginable success, was somewhat precarious: The Beatles were tight as a group, not just musically, they were almost socially impenetrable. If they could fire Pete, why not him? This insecure feeling is something Ringo is reported not to have shaken off for a couple of years. More recently we have Reni's departure from the Stone Roses — after all, *Fool's Gold* was all about great rhythm section playing, and minus the drums..? Then consider the unenviable position Kenny Jones found himself in — if there was one defining element of The Who's music, more then their music even, it was Keith Moon, his playing, like his character, larger than life itself. It's not that Kenny's no good, or that Moon himself was a technical master, but that Keith pretty much was The Who. Even Simon Phillips' later tenure with the group wasn't quite right.

Many bands, deprived of their drummer, elect not to carry on — Bill Berry's recent aneurysm meant that REM's world tour stopped dead in its tracks. You do wonder, given that drummers lend so much personality to an outfit, how some bands can change drummers quicker than Liz Taylor changes husbands. The endless procession of players through The Cult, The La's, any band that hires Cozy Powell, and the fact that Nirvana took ages to settle on Dave Grohl almost defies belief.

At the centre of this lies a bizarre contradiction: to most, drums are (apparently) easy; all you have to do is hit them, therefore any idiot can do it. This is an opinion that seems to affect even the finest musicians. So the drummer, often enough, is the last consideration in piecing together a band. We've all seen *The Commitments*, but you know and I know that the drummer is pretty much central to how well a band works. Drummers can single-handedly propel bands by sheer personality alone, and to us drummers this is the most obvious thing in the world. But take heart, the chances are if you're taking someone's place in a band it's because they want you and your inimitable style, flair, panache and large car. That or it's something else. After all, at the end of *Piss Off Pete* the interviewer says, "So, do you reckon they took on Ringo because he had better drugs than you?"

# chapter 14
## See You In Court

It's undoubtedly true that man's first creative instrument was percussive, so why is it that so many drummers today still encounter the unfair criticism that they don't contribute to the writing of a song? Maybe it's because, as drummers, we're really nice types who just love helping people out with their writing projects for no personal gain. More probable is sheer ignorance and naiveté on the one hand, and more than a fair portion of ego on the other.

I'd been playing drums professionally for fifteen years only to find myself expelled from a band because I'd disputed my lack of credit. I needed to have this question addressed, otherwise how could I dedicate myself to an instrument and career that would always prevent me from being credible. My need was so great that I was prepared to go all the way to the High Court if necessary to get some answers — and some of those answers were pretty enlightening.

Before I get into the legalities, I think it would be wise to briefly describe my situation as it was.

I'd joined a band on invitation and within six months we had collaborated on repertoire of about 12 songs. By collaborated, I mean we all played together in room with our instruments and, together, worked out our respective parts until we were happy that we'd achieved our sound. The singer would formulate the lyrics around the music we'd created. We'd managed to get a lucrative deal with a well known record label for a possible five albums worth of material. Unfortunately, as all the hype grew leading up to the deal (and let's face it, you can hear people talking hundreds of thousands of pounds), so did our singer/guitarist's ego. He'd decided that he was the sole writer of all the material, based on the theory that if he wrote the lyrics and the melody he delivered them with, then he's written the entire song and he alone should be credited accordingly. I seemed to be the only group member who was prepared to dispute this point openly. After secretive discussions in my absence, I was informed that I was to be expelled from the band under the pretext of personal differences. Unfair enough, you might think, but what made it worse was the fact that we'd all signed a recording contract (something I'd also been instrumental in achieving) which meant substantial amounts of money were imminent, not to mention the great opportunity to have the band recorded and marketed to the public.

So much for the 'brotherhood' I was supposed to have joined; I wasn't even being considered a distant relative. All that was on offer to me now was one quarter share of the second-hand value of all the recently purchased guitar equipment, in return for my signature waiving all my rights to the songs and any claims I might have against the other members.

I took immediate legal advice and prepared my claim for a declaration that I was entitled to share in the copyright of the various musical works, and for an account of what was due to me as a result of the termination of the partnership between us. Within the legal exchanges that took place, the band changed its stance by saying that the agreement between us was only an agreement between players, and not writers — although the bass player was now credited as co-writing one of the songs, and the lead guitarist with co-writing another. Meanwhile, I was still just a drummer, and so, presumably, not creditable.

So that's how it stood, and all parties were prepared to go to court to have the stalemate judged. After a considerable length of time we met again in the High Court.

## THE ISSUES

**1.** *What was my fair credit, if any, for my creative involvement? (What was the legal test that must be satisfied before I could claim joint authorship within the meaning of the Copyright Act 1956?)*

**2.** *What was the relationship between myself and the other members of the band? In particular, was there, in law,*

*a partnership between us?*

**3.** *If there was a partnership, what was the effect in law of the 'termination' of the partnership?*

## THE LEGAL PRINCIPLES
**1.** *Section 11(3) of the 1956 Copyright Act provides that:*

*"Work of joint authorship means a work produced by the collaborations of two or more authors in which the contribution of each author is not separate from the contribution of the other author or authors."*

*This subsection was reproduced in section 10(1) of the 1988 Act whereby the word 'distinct' has replaced the word 'separate'. The judge commented that for the present purposes the following test is appropriate:*

*"In the absence of any express agreement, if two or more people collaborate with each other, and, with a common design, produce an original musical work, they will be treated as joint authors under the act."*

*He then went on to say:*

*"There is no copyright in ideas. Thus, a person with an original idea is not the author or copyright owner of any work composed by another who make use of that idea, unless the person with the idea contributes to the 'form' in which copyright exists."*

*After listening to evidence given, the judge said:*

*"On my finding of fact, after the plaintiff had joined the group, the band sat down with their instruments and, by common design, composed pieces, each of them making his own contribution to the whole piece in such a way that the individual contribution could not be separated from one another. Composing was a joint enterprise and was treated as such by the group and was for their*

*mutual benefit. Accordingly, I am satisfied that the plaintiff has proved an entitlement to 25% copyright in the music of the songs."*

**2.** *On the relationship question, the judge concluded:*

*"When the band started, they shared their profits and losses. They were professional musicians and formed the group for the purpose of making money. That being so, the only conclusion that can sensibly be drawn is that they were in partnership with each other trading under the name of the group."*

*Having won this last point, the remaining question was relatively easy to resolve.*

**3.** *The judge said:*

*"In my judgement, the members of the group were partners and that partnership dissolved when the plaintiff was expelled. The plaintiff is entitled to an account of the moneys which are due to him. Those moneys will include a sum to represent his quarter share of the assets of the partnership at that time and such rights as he may have under section 42 of the Partnership Act of 1980."*

The judge also noted that the fact that installments of substantial sums of money were due under the recording contract made the assets of the partnership at that time more valuable. He then ordered:

"The taking of all necessary amounts and enquiries as between plaintiff and the defendants arising from the dissolution of their partnership at that time, and from the exploitation of the songs of which the plaintiff holds 25% of the copyright to the music."

## IN MY VIEW

To analyse what was awarded:

In copyright or authorship I'd been awarded 25% of the music to the songs written while I was a member of the band. If you reduce copyright of a song to a percentage, the lyrics or words take 50% of the song's copyright, and the remaining 50% is then awarded to the music. Our music was written between all four of us, so I was awarded 25% (or one quarter) of the 50% copyright awarded to the music. This system gives each player 12.5% in the songs. The singer, however, gained a further 50% copyright which is awarded to the lyrics or words. Therefore, he should receive $50 + 12.5 = 62.5\%$ copyright or authorship in the songs. Still a substantial amount and yet all parties have received fair compensation for their creative investment. Of course, not all singers write their own lyrics and in that case the equation might differ, but the basis of a song being words and music, $50\% + 50\%$, should keep members satisfied.

One important lesson to be learned is that matters such as this inevitably come down to fact and degree, but if somebody wants to retain control of all the copyright of a song then they should have something already recorded or written to guide what you play. If this is so, then really you have little or no investment and a fee should be applicable, unless you feel charitable.

All too often, musicians who may be in the early stages of their career doubt or don't realise their worth. It doesn't matter how naive your playing might be, it is still creative and can still make a song quirkily or strangely attractive. I'm writing from a drummer's point of view, but these issues inevitably affect every musician.

It's unfortunate that there are still people out there who are all too willing to discard drummers when it comes to a writing credit. If more drummers, indeed musicians, would realise their worth, maybe we could put an end to what is still a major problem.

There are lots of fair-minded, sincere and honourable musicians out there to play with, the luck is in finding them.

# chapter 15
# Borrowed Time

Drummers stick together, that's what drummers like to say. Now while it has always struck me as (possibly) rather sad that drumming should be all some people have in common, and that it can serve negatively in reinforcing the idea amongst other musicians that we batteurs live in some sad, hickory-fixated, nylon-tipped ghetto, it is nevertheless a source of pride that seems to lift us in our darker hours. But there are limits to my willingness to be part of this league of gentlefolk, aside from the wearing of gratuitous Zildjian caps — fair enough if you're Manu Katché, but are you? No, no you're not. No, my primary limit is kit sharing. Forget brotherhood, fraternity, all pulling together — I don't like it one bit. Not to say I don't indulge in a spot of it myself, but I don't like it one bit.

You know the scene: you get to the gig and someone shambles up to you, saying, "How do you feel about sharing?" A while back — before I got really busy and the only times my kit saw the light of day were very, very rare — these words alone would make me splutter with incandescent rage. "No," I'd say, "I'm not sharing with anyone." I don't care how many pints they try to buy me — don't they realise I'm driving? I mean, of course I am, I brought my kit! So no way

is he (or she) using my kit. No! Dammit, no! I'd then proceed to try and put off the drummer in question: "Oh you won't like the way I've tuned it; the stool's very low/high/got razor blades in. I like it like that..." In fact I'd say anything to avoid having to share.

But why? It's territorial. Because a drum kit is, in a way, like your bedroom, your own personal turf — you sit here, you set it up your own way (usually in your actual bedroom for *&@!'s sake), you picked those cymbals, you cracked those cymbals, why should anyone else bloody have 'em? Eh? Eh?! The cheek of it. And it's worse, much worse, when they don't bring their own pedals or snare drum — this to me is the collapse of all civilised courtesy — you've never met this person and here they are intruding in a way you never expected when you first arrived at the gig.

Hang on, you're saying, it can't all be down to me being finicky about manners. There are of course plenty of rational excuses I can rack up. For a start, there's the way you've tuned your kit — it's aimed to blend in with/stand out from the way the band you play in sounds; therefore it stands to reason that it won't be what another band wants. Though having said that I have to say that any helpful engineer will see to that anyway, more of which later. Often enough when I get to a gig I am horrified/fascinated by the way another drummer has tuned his kit — if only because it's not what I'd do, or worse still it's something I've never thought of myself. So having to share mutates into an artistic ordeal the likes of which few of us could ever experience and emerge from unscarred.

No-one else is expected to have to go through this, are they? After all, have you met many guitarists willing to share? Don't bother, the way they fawn over their pedals is answer enough I'm sure; and when it comes to amps, oh darling! No! Yet the uncomprehending stares you get when you say you're unkeen to share are par for the course.

Why are things like this? While of course it's a glorious act of brotherhood to let someone else play your kit, it's a lazy, disorganised, unbrotherly arse who asks you in the first place. Or it's someone who has quite simply faced reality, woken up and smelt the coffee. With most clubs there's really no point in bringing anything more than a bass and a snare (and maybe a hi-hat), as that's all that's going to be miked up. All too often the sum effect of going round the toms in a climactic fill is to vanish altogether like a sonic submarine beneath the ice only

to resurface at the beginning of the bar. No wonder so many seasoned club drummers have four-piece kits or less — the rest is a waste of time and effort. How you tune your toms, while a matter of taste, is nevertheless sonically irrelevant, so why not share? You can have as broad a pallet as you like, but stages are so tiny that all it takes is everyone to turn up with a kit and there's no room for anyone else — bassists, guitarists, whatever. Sometimes it actually helps if someone doesn't bother bringing a kit. Of course, although it's never happened to me, there is always the danger that everyone turns up without a kit... Maybe that's what inspired the man who gave us the drum machine.

But as I hinted at the top of the page, I do share. Oh yes. In fact lately I've been the one shambling up to the poor bloke who's bothered bringing his kit and asking if I can use it. I always bring a snare, I always bring my pedals, I usually bring my cymbals too. The thing is, I've faced reality on this one; and not only that, you know that the headliner will lend you their kit, and that it's going to get decent sound check, and I don't give a shit what it sounds like. I didn't have to lug the bastard here. And that's why I'm all for drummers as a band of brothers, and why if you want to borrow mine you can — because who knows, one day I may need to borrow yours.